T0195718

GODLY
DISCONTENTMENT

MICHEE FERDINAND

WESTBOW
PRESS®
A DIVISION OF THOMAS NELSON
& ZONDERVAN

WestBow Press books may be ordered through booksellers or by contacting:

WestBow Press
A Division of Thomas Nelson & Zondervan
1663 Liberty Drive
Bloomington, IN 47403
www.westbowpress.com
1 (866) 928-1240

ISBN: 978-1-9736-0117-3 (sc)
ISBN: 978-1-9736-0116-6 (hc)
ISBN: 978-1-9736-0118-0 (e)

Library of Congress Control Number: 2017913885

Print information available on the last page.

WestBow Press rev. date: 09/12/2017

But I have this against you
That you have left your first love
Rev.2:4(NAS)

Worship our Heavenly Father is certainly the most important topic in all time.But when it is the Lord who has something against the Church, it is not a laughing matter, it's time to tremble. However, As long as the love is more important than the disappointment, you can work out just about any problem between you. It is only when disappointment seems more important than love that relationship problems become toxic.

"Go and proclaim in the ears of Jerusalem, saying, " Thus says the Lord, I remember concerning you the devotion of your youth, the love of your betrothals, your following after Me in the wilderness, through a land not sown (Jer.2:2}NAS

CONTENTS

ACKNOWLEDGMENTS

Thanks to my Lord and Savior Jesus Christ

This project would have been impossible without the inspiration of the Holy Spirit. I am so thankful that God uses me through a book to write and emphasize the complaint about the unending love of God on you and me. God will never give up on trying to help you understand how deep His love for you is. I hope this book will be as much of a blessing for you to read as it has been for me to write. This book is not necessarily prescriptive. It is descriptive of the worship practices throughout the church age as related to our knowledge and our comprehension of the Word of God. I pray that you would understand how these truths can transform your walk with God as I struggled to embrace the peace that comes from the perfect love of God.

Special thanks to my wife Ramona, who I have learned to love and cherish through the stormy time. It wasn't by accident that God brought you into my life during this special time

Also to my siblings other parents and friends. You all have a huge impact on my life and I love you. I never imagined in such occasion you would be an outstanding source of encouragement and comfort to me.

However, if you wish to be on good terms with God, and have his grace direct your life, and come to the joy of love, then fix this name "Jesus" so firmly in your heart that he never leaves your thought.

For by the grace given me
I say to every one of you:
Do not think of yourself
more highly than you ought,
but rather think of yourself
with sober judgment,
in accordance with the faith
God has distributed to each of you.
(Rom 12:3 NIV)

FOREWORD

The World under the control of Satan is filled with many kind of philosophy empty imaginable deception. And people by the million are buying into this false system. The Great Deceiver is not satisfied with that, He is also after the believers' minds. Knowing that He can't interfere with our salvation because the ransom price has being paid in consideration of which we are set free. God secures our redemption by the payment of that ransom. He loved us, and He proved it by the purchase of our souls. The Bible explains it clearly, when we walk away from the will and the word of God, we walk toward death. I am referring to spiritual death. Our attitude displeases God badly … And what happened to our first love?

The leaders can't take any higher morally, ethically than they've been themselves. The flock has been neglected. It involves the development of a daily discipline of studying the word, so they will be equip to lead the church. Therefore, lack of awareness makes us loose our identity. Anything that displeases, and saddens God catches our attention. It's not a laughing matter at all. I would call it a disgrace.

God wants His children to have a revival in their hearts. He knows about our daily struggle with sin that's why the Bible reminds us that we are saved by His grace. In spite of what the Lord had and continued doing for us we choose to walk in the darkness of the world. What happened to our first love?

The purpose of written this book is to pursue the believers to make an about-turn and go back to the Lord. The writer emphasized on the Lord discontentment and His expectation from his children. We have let Him down big time. The writer also explained how the believers had indulging themselves in many idolatries that made them failed our Heavenly Father. Repent! Stop crushing our Creator's heart and His love will redirect you to the right way. Go back to the Old Practice, from there, you will be more focused, enjoyed the Peace and regained the perfect love that we only find in Jesus. Let one, and all get serious about our salvation, for it is later than we think. May our Merciful God Bless you tremendously, and show you the way to find His love.

Ramona M. Ferdinand

INTRODUCTION

Certain authors, speaking of their works, say, 'my book,' my commentary,' 'my history,' etc. They resemble middle class people who have a house of their own, and always have 'my house' on their tongue. They would do better to say, 'our book, "our commentary, our history," etc., because there is in them usually more of other people's than their own. Pascal, Pensees, #43 (1)

All books have a viewpoint as the author is seeking to communicate an idea or story they care about or consider important. With the help of some evangelical authors and others, I have focused my attention on the complaint that brought into existence this book that raised the important issue of our modern and sophisticated lifestyle in our personal, family, community,social and specially church lifestyle.

"In God we trust"

What a powerful logo, certainly the world recognizes the importance of the preeminence of God in the life of our forefathers and our fathers. As we will see in the pages that follow the reason that justified the discontentment and the complaint of our heavenly father

This book is central to an understanding of spiritual personal, social and cultural life in the story of Christianity in America and all over the world. Surely this epistle has its lessons for us whether as a religious community or as individuals. Before we consider the complaint, let's ask a question: what is all about?

The first love/ the best love (*Agape)*

"Whom else have I in the heavens? None beside you delights me on earth (Psa 73:25 NAB)" *is the language of every heart, when its love of God is true in principle and supreme in degree.*

Tragically, many forgeries are accepted by believers day after day and then sold to others in the Christian marketplace as authentic love or the will of God for us. They in turn neglect and distort the will of God through a mechanical orthodoxy. In our society we try desperately to set aside anything unpleasant. Sometimes we even end up putting make up over unpleasant scriptures

In this book, I spotlighted what I believe is the major factors of our age. It is not liberalism or modernism, nor the old Roman Catholicism or the new Roman Catholicism, nor the threat of communism, nor even the threat of rationalism, intellectualism and traditionalism consensus which surrounds us. All these are dangerous but not the primary threat. The real problem is this: "**we have left our first love**" the church of the Lord Jesus Christ, individually or corporately, tending to do the Lord's work in the power of the flesh rather than of the Spirit. The central problem is always in the midst of the people of God, not in the circumstances surrounding them.

The late Francis Schaeffer once observed that "the meaning of the word Christian has been reduced to practically nothing ...... Because the word Christian as a symbol has been made to mean so little, it has come to mean everything and nothing"

The term Christian in contemporary usage can mean anyone who is not Jewish, anyone who lives in a "Christian" nation (as opposed, for example, to a Buddhist or an Islamic one), or anyone who claims any kind of allegiance to Jesus Christ. But though the world may be confused about what a Christian is, the Bible is clear. Christians are those who are united to God through saving faith in Jesus Christ and who are thus members of His body, the Church.(2)

I

VISUALIZATION

*You will find as you look back upon your life that the
moments when you have really lived are the moments
when you have done things in the spirit of love.*

Henry Drummond

How can we best understand the discontentment of God?

For centuries, by word of mouth, the record of our trespass was to be passed down through ages, by elders to children, until with the invention of writing, the story of redemption could be put down on dried sheepskin and so preserved up to date through technology. In many ways the book of Revelation picks up themes that start in Genesis and brings them and others to a focus.

As the matter of fact, the voice of God is always speaking to us, and always trying to get our attention. But his voice is a "still, small voice" and we must at least slow down in order to listen. Keep looking to God, keep trusting in him. Know that he is always leading you to a higher place. Let him take control of your life. The road may look strange to you. You may even feel lost, or far behind, or confused. Sometimes, despite our best intentions, we find ourselves wandering in a wilderness of anxiety, lost and unable to find our way out. But if you follow Jesus, it will be the right road, and in the end you will have peace. For peace is found only in the center of God's will

Who are we?

We are the Bride of Christ, sinners saved by Grace, united in one Body, by one Spirit, for the sole purpose to live and have our being in Christ, throughout the ages of time and eternity, to the Glory of God the Father!

We are Christians, we're the called out ones-who have been separated from out of the world by God, cleansed from all sin through the shed blood of the Lamb of God, and given a new nature in Christ.

His divine power has bestowed on us everything that makes for life and devotion, through the knowledge of him who called us by his own glory and power. Through these, he has bestowed on us the precious and very great promises, so that through them you may come to share in the divine nature, after escaping from the corruption that is in the world because of evil desire. (2Pe 1:3-4 NAB)

We have not only been called by Him unto glory, but we have been made partakers of His Divine Nature, and have escaped the corruption that is in the world through lust.

Our mission

The church has a Spiritual purpose

The local church or assembly of believers has different roles that God gave to specific believers for the purpose of perfecting or training the believers, doing the work of the ministry, and strengthening of the church body

(Ephesians 4:11-14)." **11** And he gave some as apostles, others as prophets, others as evangelists, others as pastors and teachers," (Eph 4:11 NAB)

The roles given in the Bible are apostles, prophets, evangelists, pastors, and teachers. Deacons are also mentioned in Acts 6:1-7 and 1Timothy 3:8-13 as servants to wait upon people with physical needs.

The church body also serves as a local group to worship, praise and resolve conflicts

(Matthew 18:15-20)

v.**15** "And if your brother sins, go and reprove him in private; if he listens to you, you have won your brother. (Mat 18:15 NAS) and serve as a court (1 Corinthians 6:1-8)." **1** How can any one of you with a case against another dare to bring it to the unjust for judgment instead of to the holy ones? (1Co 6:1 NAB) In addition, baptisms and the Lord's Supper or communion are observed by the church body (Acts 2:37-40; 1 Corinthians 11:17-34).

Depending on the size of the church body, other ministries are performed by the members of the church as God has gifted each person (Romans 12:3-13; Ephesians 4:1-8). **"1** I, then, a prisoner for the Lord, urge you to live in a manner worthy of the call you have received," (Eph 4:1 NAB)

God wants believers in Christ to live in the midst of a corrupt culture. That's what the church is aiming for. No matter how hard we try to get ourselves loose. God does not let go. That doesn't mean he controls everything we do. It doesn't mean he puts a bridle on us and leads us by the nose. He gives each one of us free will and common sense and a spirit that can communicate with his. When we go through temptation and afflictions, he allows us to choose our response. But no matter what our response may be, he sticks around to the bitter end.

In spite of all that God has done for us in Christ we still have a problem. How do we translate our eternal position in Christ to our every day practice? How do we live Christ in our daily life?

We still have a daily struggle with sin. We are called upon to make daily decisions that affect our relationship with Christ. In most situations, we do not make a long analyzed decision whether to sin or not to sin. We don't get up one Monday morning and decide we are going to throw away our Christian life. It is usually quick, flash of the moment of poor judgment and the deed is done.(1)

Therefore, we have a problem!

The problem is clearly defined by the apostle Paul:

"I am of flesh." "Flesh" is the material from which our human nature is composed. It is the weaker element in human nature. Watch and pray that you may not undergo the test. The spirit is willing, but the flesh is weak." (Mat 26:41 NAB) Rom. 6:19; 8:3). The apostle Paul also describes it as the unregenerate state of men (Rom. 7:5; 8:8-9). " For while we were in the flesh, the sinful passions, which were *aroused* by the Law, were at work in the members of our body to bear fruit for death." (Rom 7:5 NAS)

The "flesh" is that weaker nature within us that responds to the downward pull of sin. It is in opposition to God and all that which pleases Him. It is the unregenerate state of man.

The Apostle Paul says, "I am sold under sin" (KJV, NIV). The NASB reads, "I am sold into bondage to sin." The word for sold [pipraskoμ] is a verb to sell. It is perfect tense emphasizing the state of completion, or condition. It has been sold. A. T. Robertson notes, "Sin has closed the mortgage and owns its slave."

Indwelling sin pulls, like a master demanding servitude even though the mind longs to be free. The Law fulfils its spiritual purpose because it reminds me of a daily war. I am a believer, but I am not perfect. See if you can't identify with what Paul is saying here. "For what I am doing, I do not understand; for I am not practicing what I would like to do, but I am doing the very thing I hate. But if I do the very thing I do not want to do, I agree with the Law, confessing that the Law is good" (vv. 15-16). We are saints who sin. I fail to do what I know will please God (v. 15, 19a, 22). I want to do what is right and I don't do it. In my inner man, I want to serve Christ. "I am not practicing what I would like to do." In verse 19a, "For the good that I want, I do not do." I do the very thing I hate (vv. 15-16, 19b-23). "I am doing the very thing I hate." "I practice the very evil that I do not want" (v. 19b). In my flesh I want to serve self. I want to please my selfish desires. I want to make myself look good.(2)

Despite the prominence given in the exploration of human self-understanding, the literally language bears eloquent witness to our shortcomings. From theological viewpoint, humanity is to be comprehended as rebellious and complex but in the same time in the process, sometimes for the best, many times for the worst. Then one of the two things happens: we struggle or we yield to the Spirit.

Believers responsibility

Now those who belong to Christ [Jesus] have crucified their flesh with its passions and desires. (Gal 5:24 NAB)

Galatians 2:19 and 6:14 say that Christians have been crucified with

Christ, but 5:24 says that themselves have acted to put to death their sinful nature. Believers are responsible to crucify their sinful nature. Since Roman crucifixion was a merciless, painful means of execution, Paul's statement describes an absolute and irreversible renunciation of evil. (3)

The bottom line is, as human beings we are created in the image of God, as the matter of fact, this implies that we are like God in a unique way. We can have a true knowledge of God that goes beyond mere information and relating to Him personally." Now this is eternal life, that they should know you, the only true God, and the one whom you sent, Jesus Christ". (John 17:3 NAB)

What a shock a dramatic situation to be told that you don't love Christ as you once did! So the imagery here is very strong.

It is easy for all of us to succumb to the popular, secular way of thinking and loving God. So many of us because of our ignorance, we constantly seek His face and try to understand how He wants us to love Him and to live according to His Word even if it is in conflict with our culture. The letter to the church of Ephesus clearly states the dissatisfaction of God.

Meanwhile, God is love and He is in love with His people. "His goodness is beyond our ability to comprehend, but not our ability to experience. Our hearts will take us where our heads can't fit."(4)

However, God gives us dominion over everything, including the flesh. That we are capable of being holy if we really submit ourselves to His will according to Eph.3:20-21 …"

Now to Him who is able to do exceeding abundantly beyond all that we ask or think, according to the power that works within us, 21 to Him be the glory in the church and in Christ Jesus to all generations forever and ever. Amen (Eph 3:20-21 NAS)

May God's eternal Love and magnificent plan for all the ages past and yet to come including His personal desire that you will come to know Him and be found in Christ, in whom to know is life eternal, become a reality.

(Motivation verse):

We also know that the Son of God has come and has given us discernment to know the one who is true. And we are in the one who is true, in his Son Jesus Christ. He is the true God and eternal life. (1Jo 5:20 NAB) (5)

God assumes full responsibility for our needs when we obey Him.

1 Cor.14:33 & 40 set the rules for his church and Dr Charles F Stanley explain it very well in his life principles bible.

For God is not *the author* of confusion, but of peace, as in all churches of the saints. (1Co 14:33 KJV)

God is not the author of confusion but of peace. The church is a living organism that is constantly growing and changing. Yet it does so in an organized, obedient, godly fashion— not in chaos. God does not tell one person to do something that completely contradicts and invalidates what He told someone else to do. Nor does He ever command anything that is in opposition to His eternal Word. He is the Lord of order, so when He brings us into fellowship with the rest of His church, He has special plans to use our gifts and talents within that group, and He keeps us unified with the rest of the body through His Holy Spirit.

Let all things be done decently and in order. (1Co 14:40 KJV) Confusion is never a sign of God's leading. When something spirals out of control, you can be sure that He did not design it. He may lead us in unusual ways, but He will never guide us in a manner inconsistent with His holiness and Word.

Since the church is a living organism that is constantly growing and changing, we have to face the reality.

"Whether we are trained in psychology or not, we have a strong need to make sense of our world, a strong need to know and understand what is going on around us. If we understand the world around us, we have a far greater chance of controlling it. Even if we can't control our world, understanding can help us to make informed choices about what to do next. So we are constantly analyzing situations, trying to predict the behavior of others and pinpoint answers to questions such as Who am I? And what is my purpose?

We have a strong need to know and a strong need to eliminate uncertainty. Arie Kruglanski has devoted his career to studying the lengths to which humans will go in order to avoid ambiguity. He studies a phenomenon called our need for cognitive closure, which is defined as an individual's "need for a firm answer to a question, any firm answer as opposed to **confusion and/ or ambiguity.**" (6)

It makes no difference how much we talk about our love if we do not obey Christ.

But even though we, or an angel from heaven, should preach to you a gospel contrary to that which we have preached to you, let him be accursed. (Gal 1:8 NAS)

From my first book titled "Confusing in Between " pages 13-14 theologically, I described what we are supposed to know and understand about orientation. This is another way to detect the spirit of confusion or ambiguity under the cover of ignorance or intellectualism in the body of Christ as a chosen people. It is obedience that counts, not words. Obedience without love is theoretically possible, but love without obedience is, in practice, impossible. It is a satanic substitute for God's plan. I pray that whoever reads these pages, will find a God-inspired word in the midst of this dramatic situation.

Ignorance is an unguarded door for the enemy to come through unawares, so we need to learn how to guard the door to our faith like the Bereans did. We can judge doctrine by the Word of God, and we're required to test ourselves to see if we're in the faith.(7)

Also the current false beliefs of many "so called" theologians and their often-repeated expression "all truth is God's truth". If you have even thought this way momentarily my friend you have succumbed to an intellectual temptation brought about by that same serpent (the Devil) who tempted Adam & Eve in the garden. (8)

In order to understand the main reason of God's discontentment, let's visualize the church of Ephesus as first family and the subject of his frustration, God's heart is crushed with grief and disappointment.

1 "To the angel of the church in Ephesus write: The One who holds the seven stars in His right hand, the One who walks among the seven golden lampstands, says this:

2 'I know your deeds and your toil and perseverance, and that you cannot endure evil men, and you put to the test those who call themselves apostles, and they are not, and you found them to be false;

3 and you have perseverance and have endured for My name's sake, and have not grown weary.

4 'But I have this against you, that you have left your first love. (Rev 2:1-4 NAS)

God's Definition of Love

Love without divine definition (God's revealed channels within which it must flow) becomes the most horrible thing on earth. It can destroy human beings by the millions, and can be reduced to satanic sentimentalism.

Love, as defined by God, is doing for a person that which is best for him in the light of eternity, no matter what the cost may be. That is how God defines it. Somehow, when it comes to world evangelism, many people have forgotten God's definitions and have fallen into sentimentalism.

Consider some key Scriptures that illustrate the distinction between Love and Truth.

31 Jesus then said to those Jews who believed in him, "If you remain in my word, you will truly be my disciples,

32 and you will know the truth, and the truth will set you free." (Jonh 8:31-32 NAB)

Ultimate freedom may only be achieved by total submission—unconditional surrender to Truth.(9)

Truth

There are many who speak glowingly of their love for Jesus Christ and for lost men. In John 14:15, 21, 23,24, Jesus stresses that obedience to Truth is the best form of love: "If you love Me, you will keep My commandments. He who has My commandments and keeps them, he it is who loves Me; and he who loves Me shall be loved by My Father, and I will love him, and will disclose Myself to him." Jesus answered and said to him, "If anyone loves Me, he will keep My word; and My Father will love him, and We will come to him, and make Our abode with him. "He who does not love Me does not keep My words; and the word which you hear is not Mine, but the Father's who sent Me (NAS)

This is what we call the acid test of love—does a man obey the commandments of the Lord Jesus Christ?

When we first come to Christ, every believer is on fire with thankfulness. But through the natural process of life, work, raising children, and whatever else may captivate your attention, it is easy to lose that deep sense of thankfulness. So believers feel strong because they have grown and hit a plateau on their walk. But there are no plateaus, only the constant, upward call of Christ Jesus. (10)

The act of adopting a common identity that supersedes all other identities is a daunting, even painful, one. However, research shows that it is the key to true unity. It is consistent with Jesus' teachings that the household of God is to take precedence over all other households.

Rodney Clapp writes, "Jesus creates a new family. It is the new first family, a family of his followers that now demands primary allegiance. In fact, it demands allegiance even over the old first family, the biological family." To embrace our identities in this new, common family, we must engage in the difficult process of lessening our grip on the identities that we have idolized and clung to for far too long. In many ways, this process will jar our souls, wreaking havoc on the satisfyingly homogenous existence in which we are rooted. At first, it will feel painfully unnatural because we have lived outside of our true identities for so long that the truth seems wrong. I guarantee you that we will want to quit. (11)

IT'S ALL ABOUT LOVE

"Go and proclaim in the ears of Jerusalem, saying, " Thus says
the Lord, I remember concerning you the devotion of your
youth, the love of your betrothals, your following after Me in
the wilderness, through a land not sown (Jer.2:2}NAS

Through apocalyptic letter, John communicated the same message of love to the church at Ephesus. Perhaps you could benefit of it by considering this message as an audit of your personal life and decide what you stand for and then stand for it no matter what!

"But, I have this against you

That you have left your first love"

Judah was once passionately in love with Jehovah. She was holy to Him, and anyone who troubled her experienced disaster. Now, however, as Kyle Yates puts it: The honeymoon is over. God reminds rebellious Israel of the fervor and the warmth and the purity of the love streams in the early days. She was desperately in love with her Lover and the tender love made life full of music and joy and hope. She was pure and clean and holy. No disloyalty or unclean thought marred the beauty of her devotion. But now the picture is heart-rending. God's heart is crushed with grief and disappointment. Israel now is living in open sin. She is unfaithful to the covenant vows. Other gods have stolen her affection. She has ceased to love Yahweh and her conduct is shameful in the extreme. (12)

Multi images presentations are presented to explain a variety of messages concerning the dissatisfaction of God. In general, the panoramic view can be defined as the abandonment of the first love. Let see in reach area do we need to focus in order to improve our relationship with God.

II

REAL THEOLOGY AFFECTS PRACTICE

We all know that's true. The ideas we hold in our minds, the things we take to be true, always affect the way we act and live.

Little children, let us not love with word or with tongue, but in deed and truth. (1Jo 3:18 NAS)

We love Him because He first loved us.v.19

If someone says, "I love God," and hates his brother, he is a liar; for he who does not love his brother whom he has seen, how can he love God whom he has not seen? V.20

And this commandment we have from Him: And this commandment we have from Him, that the one who loves God should love his brother also. (1Jo 4:21 NAS)

How we understand the nature and significance of the love of God affects how we act as children of God, church members and church leaders. And what we understand to be true about preaching affects how we preach and how much priority we give to preaching in our local churches.

Anyone can love in the abstract way, but John challenges us to express our love in practical terms. He repeatedly appeals for love not wishy-washy opinions that pass for truth in our society, but the absolute, eternal truths of God's word.

The Lord will often put people in our lives to mature our faith . Iron is sharpened by iron; one person sharpens another. (Pro 27:17 NAB) The process is not always pleasant, and if we fail to evaluate the situation from God's point of view, disappointment and bitterness can grow in our hearts.

But when we understand that everything that affects our lives can be used by the Lord for our good and His glory . We know that all things work for good for those who love God, who are called according to his purpose. (Rom 8:28 NAB), we learn that every relationship is an opportunity for growth and an occasion for God to express His love toward us. (1)

Accountability in the community

Obey your leaders, and submit *to them*; for they keep watch over your souls, as those who will give an account. Let them do this with joy and not with grief, for this would be unprofitable for you. (Heb 13:17 NAS)

Accountability is inescapable and inevitable because It is God working in us that enables us to do anything worthwhile for His kingdom. We obey the Lord, submit to His will and purpose, rely on His Holy Spirit who dwells within us for our every need, and please Him by giving Him all the honor and glory. Accountability to one and other is helpful and healthy. Let love be sincere; hate what is evil, hold on to what is good; (Rom 12:9 NAB) Let love be without hypocrisy. Daniel lived accountable to his peers (1-6)

People will always reflect something, whether it be God's character or some feature of the world. If people are committed to God, they will become like him; if they are committed to something other than God, they will become like that thing, always spiritually inanimate and empty like the lifeless and vain aspect of creation to which they have committed themselves. (2)

God is light, love, and life.

John enjoyed a joyous fellowship with the Lord and wanted all believers to experience the same. Unfortunately, false teachers were infiltrating the church and turning people's hearts away from Him. The church was beginning to divide over the heresy— which was likely Gnosticism— so John reminded the brethren of the foundational beliefs of the faith.

God is light. To enjoy fellowship with the Lord, we must walk in His radiance and truth. As we do so, we willingly confess our sins— allowing the blood of Christ to continually cleanse us from all unrighteousness. We must avoid embracing the lawless ways of the world and the alluring lies of false teachers.

God is love. Since we are His children, we must walk in His unconditional love. Love is more than just words; it requires action. God's unconditional love should characterize our lives. As people who have His love living within us, we need to represent Christ's authentic kindness and forgiveness to others.

God is life. Those who believe in Jesus Christ possess eternal life, and this is shown by our faithful obedience to Him. We submit to the leadership of His Spirit in full confidence that what we need, He will provide. (3)

For a better picture of what self-sacrificing love looks like, I would encourage you to carefully study 1 Corinthians 13. There are numerous misconceptions about what love is, but this one chapter in the Bible should clear them up fairly quickly. We must remember the grace and mercy that God has lovingly given us and choose to give them to others. If you want help, navigating through what 1 Corinthians 13 says about love (4)

Everything that is broken must be brought to the light of truth before it can be properly healed.

Let us therefore draw near with confidence to the throne of grace, that we may receive mercy and may find grace to help in time of need. (Heb 4:16 NAS)

God wants us to come with confidence into His presence— not timidly, anxiously, or in fear of how He might respond. He wants to help us, and He has everything we need to confront any challenge we might face. So never be afraid to approach the Father in prayer. He loves you and wants you to draw near, and because of His great mercy and grace, you can. God provides the grace we need in the hour we need it and He will provide for you too.

This may not to be an easy thing to discuss ... He created you the exact way you are for His glory and His purpose. Gary Thomas, the originator of the spiritual temperaments concept, has described these innate spiritual pathways in his book God *Sacred Pathways*: Discovering Your Soul's Path to God. He discusses nine ways to draw near to God:

- The Activist—loving God through confrontation with evil
- The Ascetic—loving God through solitude and simplicity
- The Caregiver—loving God through serving others
- The Contemplative—loving God through adoration
- The Enthusiast—loving God through mystery and celebration
- The Intellectual—loving God through the mind
- The Naturalist—loving God through experiencing Him outdoors
- The Sensate—loving God through the senses
- The Traditionalist—loving God through ritual and symbol (5)

The first thing I want to point out is that God loves His children. In fact, the very act of being called "children of God" is a way that God gives us His love. Conversely, because we are His children, He loves us. Because of this love, God has given us the amazing gift of salvation. He has pardoned the punishment we deserve for our sins and exchanged it for eternal life with Him. (6)

This subject contains theology, not the great mass of it that theologians need, but the indispensable minimum that every man needs in order that he may be living spiritually, emotionally and mentally in the real world. But you are responsible to do what you can. For each one shall bear his own load. (Gal 6:5 NAS), that's the most central issue of our lives

Jesus pointed out this very thing in the Sermon on the Mount. He knew that everyone has treasure, something that is the most important thing in his life. The main issue, he said, is where that treasure is.

"Do not lay up for yourselves treasures upon earth, where moth and rust destroy, and where thieves break in and steal. But lay up for yourselves treasures in heaven, where neither moth nor rust destroys, and where thieves do not break in or steal; for where your treasure is, there will your heart be also. (Mat 6:19-21 NAS)

What is the main point ? The point of interest is the very last sentence: *'For where your treasure is, there will your heart be also.'*

Everyone has some kind of treasure according to your personality. Everyone also has a heart - the inmost core of the self, your psychological and spiritual center of gravity. Jesus says that your heart will move to reside wherever your treasure is. In other words, you make a symbolic extension of yourself outside yourself. If your treasure is a new suit, or car, that is where your heart is.

If the boundaries of your 'self' encompass that suit or car, your sense of identity is at stake when they are damaged. Hence your disproportionate rage if soup gets spilled on your suit or your car is scratched. Ernest Becker gives the analogy of an amoeba which can extend its cell wall to surround and enclose a foreign body. A material object can become an invisible symbolic extension of my self and my identity is therefore as vulnerable as the fate of the object.

Think of the men who threw themselves off the tops of buildings when the stock market crash came in 1929. When money was their treasure, life was taken away; their heart was gone and their life became unbearable.

We can find our treasure in either of two places – in God or in something God has made on earth. We are living in a society that for the most part puts its treasure on earth; in possessions, job, status, public admiration, money, power, self-knowledge, or self-growth. We can make anything sacred. We sacralize it by giving it such importance in our priorities. (7)

You can be quite mature in your faith and still experience ignorance in the word of God. I say this because sometimes Christians believe that if they are mature in the lord, they are not going to experience alarm, or fear or shock. Those feelings are all natural human emotions, and everyone reacts differently. There are still others who truly believe that if they are mature Christians and trusting in the lord they will never experience any difficulties in their lives. Unfortunately, when these people do encounter difficulties, whatsoever, their falls apart.

As I said previously, this may not to be an easy thing to discuss. While one person may recognize that his heart for God grows stronger when he is taking a stand against evil, and another might sense that her passion for God rises most while she is sitting in a cathedral before a life-size statue of her Savior. However, our inclinations and distinctions fall into identifiable categories as I quoted previously. For example, Paul through it all, kept his faith and, as we see in romans 8, his sense of treasure, his security and his love. Human love is often fragile and easily upset. Any number of troubles can impede it. But God's love is unconditional, and once we accept His love through faith in Jesus, absolutely nothing can ever break our bond to Him

35 Who shall separate us from the love of Christ? Shall tribulation, or distress, or persecution, or famine, or nakedness, or peril, or sword?

36 Just as it is written, "For Thy sake we are being put to death all day long; We were considered as sheep to be slaughtered."

37 But in all these things we overwhelmingly conquer through Him who loved us.

38 For I am convinced that neither death, nor life, nor angels, nor principalities, nor things present, nor things to come, nor powers,

39 nor height, nor depth, nor any other created thing, shall be able to separate us from the love of God, which is in Christ Jesus our Lord. (Rom 8:35-39 NAS) (8)

III

REMEMBER

This brings up a topic that flows naturally from Genesis to our generation, regardless of era and culture. The word remember is used 170 times in the Bible. Because Jesus Christ *is* the same yesterday and today, *yes* and forever. (Heb 13:8 NAS) . His character and goodness can still be trusted. Ironically, the message is the same: ___God has created us in His image___ .That's the first love. We love, because He first loved us. (1Jo 4:19 NAS) .

In some ways, it is impossible to tackle adequately the fundamental issue of love that defines us. For emphasis, let me repeat that a different way. God has created us in His image. ___Genesis 1: 27 reads, "And God created man in His own image, in the image of God He created him; male and female He created them"___. (Gen 1:27 NAS.

Does memory speak to us in words of reproach?

Sometimes the truth hurts even as it sets you free. Who you are and you're becoming is a product of this leaving-going cycle. God crafts the character of a person using his or her experience as tools for shaping. He will do the work regardless, but He invites us to take part in our shaping and in our ministry. For some of us, let's look at the way we use to convince or touch others with our words or with whatever talent that we received from God

The zeal was so much keener. The prayers were so much more earnest. The Bible reading was so much more devout, we got so much more out of it. The presence at the Lord's Supper was so much more fruitful. Once we did love Him with all our hearts and souls. But now that love has grown less earnest, less inspiring, less uplifting. Formalism has taken the place of enthusiasm; orthodoxy there is still, but not, the old burning spirituality. We have not lost faith; we have not broken away from the creeds; we have not cast away the habits of worship; but the bright flame of 'the first love'— the love of years ago— has sunk low or gone out.

… **'Remember"** therefore from whence thou art fallen, and repent, and do the first works; or else I come to thee, and will move thy candlestick out of its place, except thou repent.' Such is the warning!(1)

Can we really think that all is right with us? We pride ourselves on our churchmanship, on our religious privileges, on our spiritual inheritance. But what of our inner lives? Authenticity is the most effective tool of communication and no amount of technique can replace it

You do it my way and I will honor you. You do it your way and you are doomed to fail. 'Let us make man in our own image, after our likeness.'

Such words absolutely exclude the idea that man, according to his original constitution, possessed anything of his own. They affirm him to be good only in so far as he reflects that which exists perfect in another, so far only as he confesses Him to be the Good. God pronounced His creation very good, because no creature was standing in itself— because the highest creature, to which all the others looked up, himself looked up to his Maker and saw his perfection in Him.

The Dutch philosopher Herman Dooyeweerd wrote, 'An image cannot be anything in itself. Man exists; that is to say, he cannot find himself except from a standpoint outside of himself, in his relationship to his Origin.' (2)

In Christian thought, the Image of God is intimately linked to the idea of Original Sin. The Image that was present in Adam at creation was partially lost with the Fall of Man, and that through the atoning sacrifice of Jesus on the cross, humans can be reunited with God. Christian writers have stated that despite the Image of God being partially lost, each person fundamentally has value regardless of class, race, gender or disability. Regardless of the exact meaning of being made in the Image of God, the concept is a foundational doctrine of Christianity and Judaism.

God's basic will for your life is not what you do or where you live or whether you marry or how much you make. It's who you become. God's primary will for your life is that you become a person of excellent character, wholesome liveliness, and divine love. (3)

But getting alone with God doesn't mean you sit in some closet and think about infinity. No, it means you get alone and discover how to be more responsible and diligent in all areas of your life. God provides unique techniques for unique person or family or people.

God really appreciated your labor, your endurance, not bearing those who are evil, testing false teachers and preachers. Feeling ready is highly overrated. God isn't looking for readiness; he's looking for the first love and **obedience.** But know who you are, accept who you are and be who you are.

A Christian's primary motive for obedience should be Love for God; it should be common sense — that is understanding that all God commandments are there for our good.

Your God-given desires serve as your basic starting point and can continue to function as a compass along the way. James Houston, author, professor, and spiritual director, says that when we come to God, we must begin where He is creating desire for Himself within us. The spiritual disciplines are only helpful as they nurture, give shape to, strengthen, and protect that desire. (4)

One of the attributes God has given us that mirrors His own, is the ability to feel emotions. God feels emotions in a way that we will never understand on this side of heaven. As a way to understand just a small taste of what God feels, He has given us our own set of human emotions. We feel joy, pain, anger, sadness, loneliness, regret, empathy, and many other complex things. The most powerful emotion we have is love. Love is the emotion that drives us to do stupid and heroic things. It propels us to desperation and pushes us to self-sacrifice.

We have been created by God as spiritual, emotional, and physical beings. Each of these parts of our being are interconnected, but also separate at the same time. As Christians we sometimes have a hard time understanding and dealing with the reality of the separateness of these parts.

Spiritual
Emotional
Physical

Spiritual/Relational Intimacy

It is extremely important that we understand spiritual intimacy because it causes most of what we struggle with and it is also a barrier to the emotional intimacy that we need. (5)

We easily recognize that spiritual problems require a spiritual solution. For example, our sin has separated us from God. God's spiritual solution of sending Jesus to die on the cross as the payment for our sin, and accepting Christ as Savior is the only way to have a relationship with God and spend eternity in heaven. There is nothing we can do physically or emotionally to get us into heaven. We have to accept God's spiritual solution to our spiritual problem of being separated from God. We have a tendency to believe that this spiritual solution should be enough to heal our physical and especially our emotional problems. It's that tendency that creates a lot of confusion for us as we try to go about dealing with our struggles. (6)

The only way to get more spiritual light is to live according to the light you have. You will know more of God's will. He will seem nearer to you. His voice will sound more clearly in your soul. You shall enter into that divine peace which the world may neither give nor take away.

Spiritual problems require a spiritual solution, physical problems require a physical solution, and emotional/relational problems require an emotional/relational solution. These parts of our being are all interconnected, so they can and do have influence over one another, and at the same time they are separate. (7)

Martin Luther King Jr said, the ultimate measure of a man is not where he stands in moments of comfort and convenience, but where he stands at times of challenge and controversy. Our personal lives are to a great extent shaped by decidedly impersonal and uncontrollable circumstances. Like it or not, sometimes bad things could be the bigger teachers in our lives. When God is in control, your mess up becomes a set up

Some people get upset about these ideas because they believe that this denies the power of God to work in someone's life when they choose to sincerely seek after Him. However, these concepts don't deny God's power in our lives, instead they call attention to how God usually chooses to apply his power in our lives. (8)

All of this is to say that regardless of different theories people with high level of differentiation have their own beliefs, convictions, directions, goals and values apart from the pressures around them. They can choose, before God, how they want to be without being controlled by the approval of others. A person behavior is nothing more than a reflection of what they truly believe deep down inside. In my point of view this is an exception and not a generality because the interior life is in constant vertical and horizontal motion.

As humans, we are on a constant search for love and acceptance. I believe that is a very specific part of the way God created us. God made us with the desire for love, because it was essential that we search for Him. As believers — now that we have found Him — we need to accept His unconditional, all-powerful, all-encompassing, merciful, and gracious love for us. So many of our confidence problems come from the fact that we do not believe God. He tells us about His amazing love for us, but we don't think this kind of love is real. Our logical, sinful heads tell us that not even God could possibly love us the way God says He does. (9)

The LORD appeared to him from afar, *saying*, "I have loved you with an everlasting love; Therefore I have drawn you with lovingkindness. (Jer 31:3 NAS)

Our lives go through seasons. Sometimes we feel close to God; at other times, especially in the midst of trials or loneliness, we may feel He is distant. But God has written us a personal letter through the Bible that is far valuable, encouraging and life changing than any note delivered by the postal service. We can read it over and over, but it's always new because it is an everlasting love. For I have said, "Lovingkindness will be built up forever; In the heavens Thou wilt establish Thy faithfulness." (Psa 89:2 NAS) " God is faithful to His promises; His love for us is eternal and unchanging.

That is the way that God feels about you. He loves you with an everlasting love, and with lovingkindness He has attempted to draw you toward Himself. If you have been resisting, please stop. It is time to enter into the joy, confidence, and security that await the children of God who understand the fullness of His love for them. (10)

No matter what we've done in the past, God has a vast amount of mercy to pour into our situation. Through the power of His Spirit God can bring back to life the devotion of your youth, the love of your bethrotals. God's love never fails.

When you trust God, and believe that His love is what makes you special and beautiful, you do not need human love to make you feel valuable. **Remember** that no other person can love you the way that God does. If you expect others to fulfill your need to be loved, you place an impossible expectation on them. Once you remove this expectation, your relationship will improve dramatically. (11)

Some of us are morning glories, and others are night owl. Choose the best time of day for you to study and meditate about the love of God. In the meantime, as you fill your mind with God's Word, consider the complaint of God about the church and yourself :

"But, I have this against you

That you have left your first love"

As Thomas states: God wants to know the real you *(with your spiritual temperament)* not a caricature of what somebody else wants you to be. He created you with a certain personality and a certain spiritual temperament. God wants your worship, according to the way he made you. That may differ somewhat from the worship of the person who brought to Christ or the person who leads your Bible study or church (12)

Spiritual Intimacy

Our model for intimacy is the picture of intimacy that we have with God. The better we know where we stand with the Lord, the stronger we can be and the stronger we are with the Lord, the more confident we will become. God automatically knows all about us. While we can't achieve that level of perfect intimacy with those around us, it should be our goal that we strive for.

Psalms 139:1-4, 23-24 is a great example of the intimacy that we have with God.

> *O Lord, Thou hast searched me and known me*
> *you know when I sit and stand; you understand my thoughts from afar.*
> *You sift through my travels and my rest; with all my ways you are familiar.*
> *Even before a word is on my tongue, LORD, you know it all.*
> *(Psa 139:1-4 NAB)*

> *Search me, O God, and know my heart; Try*
> *me and know my anxious thoughts;*

> *And see if there be any hurtful way in me, And lead me*
> *in the everlasting way. (Psa 139:23-24 NAS)(13)*

Are you comforted, as David was, by the constant presence and spiritual intimacy with God? As you look around you, do you consciously think that you deserve such attention ? God intimate knowledge of each individual confirms that we are not come together through random processes. God knows us intimately and He owns us personally and He intentionally ***created us in His image***

We need to put those precepts to work in our life. Deep intimacy with others is what God designed us for. We need intimacy with God, ourselves, and others. We can't live the abundant life alone. We also need others beyond our spouse.

Everything we have told you about (rejection, abandonment) has already happened in God's Word. God's people have been experiencing these things for a long time, and God has been taking care of His people for a long time.

That might seem to be an obvious point, but it leads to an intriguing observation. If our goal were simply to write about what God has against us, that could easily be done. The goal, therefore, is to repent as an inevitable result of the obedience and the response to the activity of God in our lives.

Believer's responsibility is to glorify God regardless of the setting or environment. Sometimes, we act as though we can bring glory to God only when the circumstances are right or, perhaps, only when we live in a setting of political or religious liberty.

So we are left with a clear choice:

The choice is frightening in its clarity. At the same time, the choice is one that every believer must make. The hope that we can somehow be obedient and return to **the first love** . The very best proof of your love for your Lord is obedience. Nothing more, nothing less, nothing else.

In summary, let us remember that humankind as the image of God has an identity rooted in and derived from the Creator. The Fall has affected us in three ways. It has spoiled our relationship to God, our re-flection of God, and our environment. Where human beings once had a close relationship with God, now there is rebellion, distrust, and unbelief.

People are personally alienated from the One who is the source of their existence. Where we once perfectly reflected the character of God in our behavior, now our lives portray a twisted and distorted likeness of him. Where once the environment perfectly matched our needs, now it is beset with disaster, sin, and death. (14)

We must remember that our very identity as Christians is that of people who have backed down before God, confessed our sin, and asked for his forgiveness instead of standing on our imagined rights or virtues. One of the most telling criticisms of Christians is that they seem to be people who say sorry - only once, at the point of their conversion, and then never again.

God himself says,: It is I, I, who wipe out, for my own sake, your offenses; your sins I remember no more. (Isa 43:25 NAB) .

And finally, in the well-known words of David,: As far as the east is from the west, so far has he removed our sins from us. (Psa 103:12 NAB.

God puts our sin away, out of arm's reach, so that it does not stand between us and him. The forgiveness of God knows no limits. Nothing is beyond his forgiveness. No sin can disqualify us from God's forgiveness as long as we come and ask God for it in humility.

Should we ignoring and disobeying God's invitation and supplication?

IV

REPENTANCE

Pay attention to the complaint of God!

Consider how far you have fallen! Repent and do the things you did at first.

Paul Tournier, the brilliant Swiss writer, physician and psychiatrist, in his splendid book "Guilt and Grace" talks about two kinds of guilt: true guilt and false guilt. False guilt, is brought on by the judgments and suggestions of man. True guilt comes from willfully and knowingly disobeying God (1)

For the sake of clarity, let's define **repentance** which is very crucial according to Sproul, R. C. So, in the most rudimentary sense, the concept of ***repentance in the Bible means*** "to change one's mind."

However, we will soon see that this is not just a matter of intellectual judgment, such as changing our approach after trying to solve a problem. Generally speaking, **metanoia** has to do with the changing of one's mind with respect to one's behavior. It contains the idea of ruing. To rue something means to regret a particular action. It carries with it not only an intellectual the experience of Old Testament Israel. When scholars examine the Old Testament understanding of repentance, they often make a distinction between two kinds of repentance. The first is cultic or ritualistic repentance and the second is prophetic repentance. (2)

If as Christians, we are commanded by our Lord to repent, we better have a good understanding of this prophetic repentance which in reality is a godly repentance. The true nature of godly repentance is found in the phrase "a broken and contrite heart, O God, you will not despise." David is saying that if he could atone for his own sins, he would; but as it is, his only hope is that God would accept him according to His mercy. Ps 51

The Bible tells us explicitly and shows us implicitly that God resists the proud and gives grace to the humble. David knows this to be true. As broken as he is, he knows God and how God relates to penitent people. He understands that God never what Jesus had in mind in the Beatitudes when He said, ""*Blessed are those who mourn, for they shall be comforted*". (Mat 5:4 NAS)* .

This text is not simply about grieving the loss of a loved one, but also the grief that we experience when convicted by our sin. Jesus assures us that when we grieve over our sin, God by His Holy Spirit will comfort us. (3)

At this point: the main complaint is: - **""But, I have this against you, says Christ, because you have left your first love"**

"Not less worthy of warning than departure from fundamental doctrine or from Scriptural morality, is the leaving of first love. The charge here is not that of falling from grace, nor that love is extinguished, but diminished. No zeal, no suffering, can atone for the want of first love." (4)

Clearly at this point, God points out the rejection or abandonment of spiritual and emotional relationship regardless of its form. Spiritual maturity and emotional health are inseparable. It is not possible to be spiritually mature while remaining emotionally immature. . *Genesis 1: 27 reads, "So God created man in His own image; in the image of God He created him; male and female He created them."* That image includes physical, spiritual, emotional, intellectual, and social dimensions. Emotionally healthy spirituality is about reality, not denial or illusion. It is about embracing God's choice to birth us into a particular family, in a particular place, at a particular moment in history. (5)

Given that the context is :"*Consider how far you have fallen! Repent and do the things you did at first."* Because for in Him we live and move and exist, as even some of your own poets have said, 'For we also are His offspring.'(Act 17:28 NAS)

What do we need to focus on, and what changes do we need to implement?

Let us look a little longer at *how far we have fallen!*

Harmful consequences occur when we forget that the lord has wired us differently and those differences are very much needed in the body of Christ. Here are just a few of the traps we can fall into when we fail to appreciate and honor one another's spiritual temperaments as indispensable gifts from God:

Judgmentalism—"Look how she's worshipping! She is so showy!"
Prescriptionism—"Just do what I do if you want to know God"
Elitism ---" My group is more spiritual than your group"
Isolationalism—"Let's start our own group where we can really pray!"
Denominationalism—"Those Bapticostals certainly don't Communion like they should" (6)

Close association with religious people, and religious worship,

We live in a broken world where many churches need to make more of an impact. This book offers a biblical and theological basis for revitalizing a church that is failing to enjoy success in its work. Understanding the biblical view of what the church is and what it is supposed to do are the key to any strategy for renewal. The search for renewal for the church must begin with a fresh look at Jesus Christ, the Lord of the church. To start elsewhere is to write the agenda for the church out of our own inadequate insights.

Jesus himself should furnish the pattern for our understanding of the church and its ministry. A renewed church, one which knows what its nature is, and is committed to its purpose, will make a difference in its corner of the world. It will truly be the salt, light, and leaven that Jesus talked about.

Worship means that God is meeting us and drawing us to Himself, that He has sent His Spirit into the world and established His Church in the world for the very purpose of bringing all to Him. This is the message that the Bible has brought to men in past ages; this is the message that it brings to them now. Rev. F. D. Maurice. (7)

Our knowledge of ourselves is at the best distorted by self-interest, ignorance and prejudice. We see in part and we know in part. Christ's knowledge is complete, objective and constructive. He rebukes so as to restore

We need to remember that the Old Testament idea of worshiping wooden, stone and metal images is still very relevant to twenty-first-century people, since we have seen that even by New Testament times, idolatry took such nonliteral forms as trusting in dead tradition or in money (recall Paul's words in Eph. 5 and Col 3). The last verse of 1 John says, "*Guard yourselves from idols.*" It is possible that he is referring to literal idols, but the church must guard itself from venerating false theology as a substitute for the true. John is saying that when we trust in false teaching, which is a false substitute for truth, then we are guilty of idol worship.

Idol worship is anything that is a substitute for worship of God. Interestingly, the Oxford English Dictionary defines "religion" as "something that one is devoted to," which can be God or something else.

Accordingly, as we have seen earlier, in the book of Revelation John refers to unbelievers as "earth dwellers," but he does not call Christians earth dwellers, even though they dwell physically on the earth. Why does he do this? John calls unbelievers earth dwellers because they are at home only here on this earth. Thus it should not be surprising to discover that of the ten times the expression occurs in Revelation, it clearly refers to idol worshipers seven times and implicitly the other three. The earth dwellers are people of earthbound vision, trusting only in some aspect of earthly security, unable to look beyond the physical things that are seen, in contrast to Hebrews 11, where Christians are called pilgrims on the earth, and they have their ultimate identity with God in heaven and in the coming new cosmos.

An idol is anything that the heart clings to for ultimate security. Accordingly, the ultimate thing in which people take security, some aspect of the world, must be destroyed. (8)

This situation drives me to take the time to address the deepest insecurities that all of us possess. I also want to answer this question and share a sincere truth with you about how our Father in heaven feels about us

Inner repentant heart.

The soul has two faculties and they should be clearly distinguished.

There is the will: its work is to love— and so to choose, to decide, to act.

There is the intellect: its work is, to know, to understand, to see: to see what—to see what's there. (9)

But there is another dimension that goes beyond our intellectual judgment named genuine repentance." It is something that is worked integral part of faith. If a person has faith but not repentance, that person does not have authentic faith. That person does not possess the necessary ingredients for redemption; conversion is a result of faith and repentance ... Genuine repentance is something that is worked in us by the Holy Spirit. It is a gracious activity by God. We have seen that conversion and repentance are inseparably linked." (10)

Modern-day readers of the Bible have a variety of reactions to the prophetic passages of Scriptures. Some find them fascinating and revealing; others find them puzzling and mysterious. Some regard them as a clearly marked roadmap for the future, others as writings whose meaning generally remains obscure. For better understanding, let's consider the prayer of Daniel as he fasted to show his sorrow and repentance for his people's sins. Daniel 9 as God foretells to Daniel the future for Israel

9:4 And I prayed to the LORD my God and confessed and said, "Alas, O Lord, the great and awesome God, who keeps His covenant and lovingkindness for those who love Him and keep His commandments,

5 we have sinned, committed iniquity, acted wickedly, and rebelled, even turning aside from Thy commandments and ordinances.

6 "Moreover, we have not listened to Thy servants the prophets, who spoke in Thy name to our kings, our princes, our fathers, and all the people of the land.

7 "Righteousness belongs to Thee, O Lord, but to us open shame, as it is this day-- to the men of Judah, the inhabitants of Jerusalem, and all Israel, those who are nearby and those who are far away in all the countries to which Thou hast driven them, because of their unfaithful deeds which they have committed against Thee.

8 *"Open shame belongs to us, O Lord, to our kings, our princes, and our fathers, because we have sinned against Thee.*

9 *"To the Lord our God belong compassion and forgiveness, for we have rebelled against Him;*

10 *nor have we obeyed the voice of the LORD our God, to walk in His teachings which He set before us through His servants the prophets.*

11 *"Indeed all Israel has transgressed Thy law and turned aside, not obeying Thy voice; so the curse has been poured out on us, along with the oath which is written in the law of Moses the servant of God, for we have sinned against Him.*

12 *"Thus He has confirmed His words which He had spoken against us and against our rulers who ruled us, to bring on us great calamity; for under the whole heaven there has not been done anything like what was done to Jerusalem.*

13 *"As it is written in the law of Moses, all this calamity has come on us; yet we have not sought the favor of the LORD our God by turning from our iniquity and giving attention to Thy truth.*

14 *"Therefore, the LORD has kept the calamity in store and brought it on us; for the LORD our God is righteous with respect to all His deeds which He has done, but we have not obeyed His voice.*

15 *"And now, O Lord our God, who hast brought Thy people out of the land of Egypt with a mighty hand and hast made a name for Thyself, as it is this day-- we have sinned, we have been wicked.*

16 *"O Lord, in accordance with all Thy righteous acts, let now Thine anger and Thy wrath turn away from Thy city Jerusalem, Thy holy mountain; for because of our sins and the iniquities of our fathers, Jerusalem and Thy people have become a reproach to all those around us.*

17 *"So now, our God, listen to the prayer of Thy servant and to his supplications, and for Thy sake, O Lord, let Thy face shine on Thy desolate sanctuary.*

18 *"O my God, incline Thine ear and hear! Open Thine eyes and see our desolations and the city which is called by Thy name; for we are not presenting our supplications before Thee on account of any merits of our own, but on account of Thy great compassion.*

19 *"O Lord, hear! O Lord, forgive! O Lord, listen and take action! For Thine own sake, O my God, do not delay, because Thy city and Thy people are called by Thy name." (Dan 9:4-19 NAS) (11)*

Therefore, repentance comprehends not only such a sense of sin, but also an apprehension of mercy, without which there can be no true repentance (Ps. 51:1; 130:4).

"I've sinned against you, and I'm sorry."

Confession and repentance isn't easy. Apologizing to another human being requires a painful amount of humility. This is why it can be a gospeling moment. When we remember what miserable sinners we are in the eyes of a holy God, there is no room left for pride. There is only one way to get to a place where you can humble yourself to the point of true repentance. You must encounter the God who left the beauty and perfection of heaven to take on skin and bones and walk beside us in our brokenness, the God who took that brokenness on Himself and was nailed to a piece of wood for it. People who have genuinely encountered that God are people consistently marked by deep humility. (12)

Once we did love Him with all our hearts and souls. But now, that love has grown less earnest, less inspiring, less uplifting. Formalism has taken the place of enthusiasm; orthodoxy there is still, but not, not, the old burning spirituality. No amount of separation, sacrifice, or service can make up for your lack of love toward the Lord. If we confess our sins, He is faithful and righteous to forgive us our sins and to cleanse us from all unrighteousness. (1Jo 1:9 NAS)

Do you wish to repent of your sins?

Ask the Holy Ghost to do it in you. Ask Him to baptize your soul with His sweet influence. It is His office and His prerogative to pour repentance into your soul. Do not dare to attempt to do it yourself without

Him! Without the Holy Ghost you may be ashamed, you may feel sorry and afraid for sin, and sin's consequence; but you will never feel the true nature and consequence of sin as grieving God and crucifying Christ! You will never be able to say, with David, 'Against Thee, and Thee only, have I sinned, and done this evil in Thy sight!'

The Lord's Complaint Against His Church 2:4

"you have left your first love"

They left their first love, they did not lose it. This was a sin of the heart, not the hand."

First love" means "best love." God wants to make you feel important. I hope you realize and discover this priceless truth for yourself and let God transform your life, body, mind and spirit, that you may love and serve Him as you should, including your neighbor

Serving Christ had become a duty instead of a joy. They had lost their intense, enthusiastic devotion for Jesus Christ (cf. John 14:23,/ 21:15-17). Do you have your "first love" for Jesus?

The Lord's Command for His Church is crystal clear :

'Remember therefore from where you have fallen, and repent and do the deeds you did at first; or else I am coming to you, and will remove your lampstand out of its place-- unless you repent. (Rev 2:5 NAS)

1. "Remember"
2. "Repent"
3. "Return"

Love can be lost, but love can be regained. (13)

V

RETURN
YOUR FIRST LOVE WILL
REDIRECT YOUR LIFE

Let the Lord have his complete way with you.
Allow God to move in you powerfully.

For then I will make pure the speech of the peoples, That they all may call upon the name of the LORD, to serve him with one accord; (Zep 3:9 NAB)

But I will leave as a remnant in your midst a people humble and lowly, Who shall take refuge in the name of the LORD-- (Zep 3:12 NAB)

Christians of African descent will be interested in Zephaniah's prophecy that the Lord would bring back his "scattered people" from "across the rivers of Ethiopia. *From beyond the rivers of Ethiopia and as far as the recesses of the North, they shall bring me offerings.* (Zep 3:10 NAB)

The context shows that Zephaniah was looking forward to the day when the Lord would bring people from the ends of the earth to become a holy people, who would worship and serve him with true hearts (3,9,12,13). Among this people would be those from "across the rivers of Ethiopia"

By the way, it is valuable to quote from "AFRO USA" a reference work on the black experience that: There are believed to be approximately 44.000 so-called "black Jews" (they are actually more appropriately classified as members of Ethiopian Hebrew congregation) in the United States. These

Jews, located in such cities as Philadelphia, Boston, Chicago, Los Angeles and New York, are mainly natives of the West Indies or the American South, although they consistently trace their ancestry and heritage back to Africa.

Closely knit, clannish, and fully involved, the black Jews continue to live successfully in poor or lower middle-class neighborhoods, despite the high crime rates prevalent in settings such as these. Both their religious optimism and the strong parental authority exercised on off-spring contribute to the inherent stability of the group. New York's Wentworth A. Matthew, leader of Harlem's Ethiopian Hebrew Congregation, credits the strength and solidarity of his group to the presence of a "towering" father figure and a tenacious mother who "sets the tone and the mood" of family life.

Like Jews everywhere, the Ethiopian Hebrew congregations observe the rituals and holidays stemming from ancient Jewish traditions. Thus, they too celebrate such joyous occasions as the liberation of the Jews from bondage in Egypt by:

Afro usa Compiled and Edited by Harry A. Ploski, Ph.D. and Ernest Kaiser Bibliographer, Schomburg Collection of reading the Passover stories and participating in the family seeder".p.908-909 (1)

Accepting God's timetable and the limitations He places on a given situation help to dispel rising anxiety. Therefore, let Him provide for you in His timing. When you accept life as a gift from the hand of God, then you will do what Helen Lemmel's song says— you will turn your eyes toward Jesus. You will look full into His glorious face and there find mercy and grace, forgiveness and hope, peace and everlasting security. What would you give to experience the peace of God? Are you willing to lay down the anger that haunts your soul because someone has done something to wound you? God knows the hurt you have experienced. Will you trust Him in quietness, knowing that He has not forgotten you but stands ready to heal you? God's peace is unshakable because there has never been a time or an event when God has felt disturbed. His peace and presence are sure. They are immovable. You will accomplish many things— great and mighty— when you keep your focus on God. (2)

If we take what happened to Paul as a kind of paradigm for Christians in general, we can assume that the Spirit of God will similarly sometimes redirect or re-shape our plans. He has many ways of redirecting us—through counselors, circumstances, His Word, His Spirit, a change in our desires, unanticipated tragedies, and a variety of other means. As we work our plans, we must be sensitive to His potential redirection.(3)

Since no one foresees his or her pathway perfectly, remain submitted to any God-given redirection to your plans. Do not brace yourself against divine redirection; rather, rejoice in it as a singular evidence of God's love, omniscience, and omnipotence. (4)

God's compassion and power are unlimited. In God's limitless mercy, He can restore or redirect our lives and bless us abundantly. We can depend on God's steadfast and attention. Because of his care, nothing in our lives happens without his awareness. Let our lives become a testimony to the people who cross our paths.

Redirection

The mind of man plans his way, But the LORD directs his steps. (Pro 16:9 NAS)

We make plans based on God's Word and thoughtful research, submit them to the Lord, proceed to work them, and then watch Him— on occasion— re-direct those very plans. The best-laid plans of godly men sometimes take a bend! (5)

My favorite passage on divine redirection comes from the life of Paul, where on one occasion during his second missionary journey the Holy Spirit rerouted him twice (Acts 16: 6-10).

And they went through the region of Phrygia and Galatia, having been forbidden by the Holy Spirit to speak the word in Asia. And when they had come up to Mysia, they attempted to go into Bithynia, but the Spirit of Jesus did not allow them. So, passing by Mysia, they went down to Troas. And a vision appeared to Paul in the night: a man of Macedonia was standing there, urging him and saying, "Come over to Macedonia and help us." And when Paul had seen the vision, immediately we sought to go on into Macedonia, concluding that God had called us to preach the gospel to them (ESV).

In order to understand the passage, we have to understand the sequence of events: --Paul attempts to enter Asia, but the Holy Spirit forbids him (v. 6). --He preaches the gospel in Phrygia and Galatia instead. –

He then heads to Mysia (v. 7). From there he attempts to enter Bithynia but the Holy Spirit stops him (v. 7). He opts instead for Troas, a coastal city of the Aegean Sea (v. 8). There he receives the "Macedonian vision" (v. 9). He concludes that God's "open door" lies across the Aegean Sea (v. 10). Why did the Holy Spirit twice redirect Paul from his chosen course of travel?

It becomes clear when the Lord opens up a large door of opportunity that he was not anticipating. This passage illustrates how divine redirection works and provides a number of helpful principles in the process. (6)

If we take what happened to Paul as a kind of paradigm for Christians in general, we can assume that the Spirit of God will similarly sometimes redirect or re-shape our plans. He has many ways of redirecting us—through counselors, circumstances, His Word, His Spirit, a change in our desires, unanticipated tragedies, and a variety of other means. As we work our plans, we must be sensitive to His potential redirection. (7)

Since no one foresees his or her pathway perfectly, remain submitted to any God-given redirection to your plans. Do not brace yourself against divine redirection; rather, rejoice in it as a singular evidence of God's love, omniscience, and omnipotence. (8)

Trusting God in the Dark

But as for me, I shall sing of Thy strength; Yes, I shall joyfully sing of Thy lovingkindness in the morning, For Thou hast been my stronghold, And a refuge in the day of my distress. (Psa 59:16 NAS)

Sometimes we have an experience in life that seems like walking through a long dark tunnel. The chilling air and the thick darkness make it hard walking, and the constant wonder is why we are compelled to tread so gloomy a path, while others are in the open day of health and happiness. We can only fix our eyes on the bright light at the end of the tunnel, and we comfort ourselves with the thought that every step we take brings us nearer to the joy and the rest that lie at the end of the way. Extinguish the light of heaven that gleams in the distance, and this tunnel of trial would become a horrible tomb. Some of us are passing through just such an experience now. (9)

The old fathers did not indeed know what has been revealed to us, but they felt that the Eternal God, in whom they believed, would never fail those that trusted Him (Psa. 34: 22).'

'The LORD bless you, and keep you; (Num 6:24 NAS).To 'keep' is to value, treasure, guard; it promises protection. The soul that trusts a merciful God will never be forsaken nor put to shame. However unworthy, ignorant, feeble or sinful, it will be protected.

GOD IS ALWAYS MAKING A WAY.

But the eyes of the LORD are on those who fear him, on those whose hope is in his unfailing love, (Psa 33:18 NIV)

When you don't have enough and you don't know where to get more; He'll make a way out of no way. You don't have to know how, when, where, or why. Just know that God is always making a way. Don't despise the little that you have. Be grateful for it. Your grateful heart is a catalyst to increase. It's a key to the door of more. Because God is always adding more to your less. He's always making a way. (10)

The Lord make His face to shine upon thee, and be gracious unto thee!' Num. 6:25-26 Like the shining of the sun after rain, like the rising sun after a black night of fear or agony; such, in the experience of God's people, is the shining of His face when the sinner beholds the atoning Savior and accepts God's offer of salvation. To him the Lord is gracious; that is, He feels and acts toward him in grace, not according to justice, but in outflowing, unmerited love, pardoning all his sins. That is the Gospel message— a loving Father, through an atoning Savior, offers pardon to every soul that will accept it and trust in Him

HIS WAYS ARE NOT OUR WAYS.

The perspective we need is not that of our neighbors, friends, co-workers or best friends. If we want to navigate life without going crazy or stressing out, we have to learn to see every situation through the eyes of God. Don't melt down, kneel down. "Rejoice always, pray without ceasing, give thanks in all circumstances; for this is the will of God in Christ Jesus for you." (1Thesselonians 5: 16-18).

In the eyes of God, what's happening is never as bad as it seems. It's working in your favor, but timing is everything. What seems like a disaster today will be a triumph tomorrow.

He can use anybody. His love transcends mistakes, mishaps, and questionable pasts. None of the people in the Old Testament or new, were perfect. You don't have to be either. Repent for your past. Turn from it. Receive the love of God and accept His forgiveness.

""*For My thoughts are not your thoughts, Neither are your ways My ways,*" declares the LORD.

"*For as the heavens are higher than the earth, So are My ways higher than your ways, And My thoughts than your thoughts (Isa 55:8-9 NAS.*

If you don't take away anything else, let Isaiah 55: 8-9 become your mantra. God does not think the way we think. He does not handle situations the way we think they should be handled. (11)

Dream may have been delayed but it was not denied.

IT SEEMS BAD BUT GOD SEES IT DIFFERENTLY.

God wants you to know that you are always on the brink of a breakthrough moment. At any given time, your circumstance can improve in a way that will make your spectators drop their bottom jaw and scratch their heads. Believe that. God wants you to know that He cares about what is happening in your life. He has your back. You are not alone. He is always with you. Even when you feel your worst, know that He is right there offering comfort and guiding you toward peace. Because He knows that in the end you will be victorious. "*But they that wait upon the LORD shall renew their strength; they shall mount up with wings as eagles; they shall run, and not be weary; and they shall walk, and not faint. (Isa 40:31 KJV)* (12)

Sometimes it is difficult to see how obscure passages, distant places, and unfamiliar symbols can have any significance for our lives. For answers we must turn not to the evening news or the front page of the newspaper, but to the Bible. God speaks to us in many ways—through the circumstances of life, through the issues of the heart, through His Holy Spirit, and in

His word. As you read this book, my prayers are that you will grow in your conviction that God is the answer to all your fears. God is our refuge when sadness and disappointment threaten to overwhelm us, but God has our best interests at heart. He is our defense in the day of trouble.

YOUR FIRST LOVE WILL REDIRECT YOUR LIFE

Love is always supportive, loyal, hopeful, and trusting. Love never fails! 1Cor. 13:7,8a. Love as God intended it is more than just passion, romantic feelings, or sentimental expressions. It involves commitment, sacrifice, service and obedience. The kind of things that benefit both the giver and the receiver.

Years ago President Theodore Roosevelt gave this penetrating call to **commitment:**

It's not the critic who counts; not the man who points out how the strong man stumbled or where the doer of deeds could have done better. The credit belongs to the man who is actually in the arena, whose face is marred by dust and sweat and blood, who strives valiantly; who errs, and comes short again and again, because there is no effort without error and shortcoming; who does actually try to do the deed; who knows the great enthusiasm, the great devotion and spends himself in a worthy cause; who, at the worst, if he fails, at least fails while daring greatly. Far better is it to dare mighty things, to win glorious triumphs even though checked by failure, than to rank with those poor spirits who neither enjoy nor suffer much because they live in a gray twilight that knows neither victory nor defeat. (13)

VI

WHAT IS THE MEASURE OF OUR INDIVIDUAL LOVE FOR HIM!

Jesus, who gave His life for us and who went through gruesome suffering for us so that we would inherit all things took time to warn us never to make the mistake of taking our calling lightly. Taking your calling for granted could have dire consequences. What did Paul write in this regard?

2 Corinthians 7: 1

Therefore, since we have these promises, dear friends, let us purify ourselves from everything that contaminates body and spirit, perfecting holiness out of reverence for God. (2Co 7:1 NIV)

Making a commitment to Christ without ever exploring what the implications of that commitment implies, is an issue that created strong reaction and division in the field of Christian community. The main point was, the contamination and the deterioration in the spiritual condition of the church. The whole dynamic of Christian life is related to our calling and implication that keep us together. I believe that there are circumstances in which honest confrontation, which all of its pain, must occur. This is true in marriage, in parent-child relationships, in friendships, and in our church life.

Do not despise the day of small things. For we do not know what is small in God's eyes. Spiritual size is not measured the same way physical size is. What unit shall we use to measure love? And yet love is real, more real than anything else. (1)

1 John 4: 11 says:" Beloved, if God so loved us, we ought also to love one another".

40

That gratitude translates in Love for God, and love for others is the measurement of our personal/relational commitment to Him." Prove that you have faith without doing kind deeds, and I will prove that I have faith by doing them" Jas 2:20 and abundant fruits which honor God and Jesus Christ.

There was a front-page article in the San Francisco Chronicle about a metro transit operator named Linda Wilson-Allen. She loves the people who ride her bus. She knows the regulars. She learns their names. She will wait for them if they're late and then make up the time later on her route.

A woman in her eighties named Ivy had some heavy grocery bags and was struggling with them. So Linda got out of her bus driver's seat to carry Ivy's grocery bags onto the bus. Now Ivy lets other buses pass her stop so she can ride on Linda's bus.

Linda saw a woman named Tanya in a bus shelter. She could tell Tanya was a stranger. She could tell she was lost. It was almost Thanksgiving, so Linda said to Tanya, "You're out here all by yourself. You don't know anybody. Come on over for Thanksgiving and kick it with me and the kids." Now they're friends.

The reporter who wrote the article rides Linda's bus every day. He said Linda has built such a little community of blessing on that bus that passengers offer Linda the use of their vacation homes. They bring her potted plants and floral bouquets. When people found out she likes to wear scarves to accessorize her uniforms, they started giving them as presents to Linda. One passenger upgraded her gift to a rabbit-fur collar. The article says Linda may be the most beloved bus driver since Ralph Kramden on The Honeymooners. (Does anybody remember old Ralph Kramden?)

Think about what a thankless task driving a bus can look like in our world: cranky passengers, engine breakdowns, traffic jams, gum on the seats. You ask yourself, How does she have this attitude? "Her mood is set at 2: 30 a.m. when she gets down on her knees to pray for 30 minutes," the Chronicle said. (2)

Emotional/Relational Intimacy with others

Emotional intimacy is one of our most basic needs. We were created by God with this need to connect emotionally and relationally with others.

Then the LORD God said, "It is not good for the man to be alone; I will make him a helper suitable for him." (Gen 2:18 NAS) (Genesis 2:18, Ecclesiastes 4: 9-12, 1 Corinthians 12: 12-26). It is also one of the needs that we find most challenging and confusing.

Many people confuse sex with intimacy. Our culture often uses the two words interchangeably. However, sex is not intimacy. A basic definition of intimacy is being fully known and fully knowing another (Psalm 139: 1-4). you know when I sit and stand; you understand my thoughts from afar. (Psa 139:2 NAB)

Being fully known requires that I become vulnerable enough to reveal all of who I am. Thoughts, beliefs, emotions, needs, and experiences are all involved in understanding what it is like to be me, including the parts of me that I fear I might be rejected for if I reveal them. Often we will experience a sense of closeness or familiarity with someone and we want to call that intimacy. Sometimes we mistake intensity for intimacy. However, we have to think of intimacy as the idea of being fully known and not just having a close, open moment or moments. The idea of being fully known by others can be a scary thought. Most of us have had the experience of revealing almost everything, but holding some parts back. We often fear that if people really knew everything, they would reject us. Sometimes we think that others really aren't that interested in knowing everything, so we share what we perceive to be the highlights, or what we anticipate the other will accept or approve of. (3)

Quite often, followers of Christ have decided to withdraw from the world and set up their own exclusive communities, or to retreat from society into "Christian Ghettos " But this does not fulfill Christ's prayer in John 17:18. *As you sent me into the world, I have sent them into the world. (John 17:18 NIV)*

Engagement, not isolation is his desire. When love will abound in you, fear will be unnecessary. You have nothing to fear. When you are filled with love, and you are busy loving, you have no time to fear.

Biblical heroes were regular people who had to learn the same things you and I have to learn — to drive out fear by increasing their knowledge of God, to shift their focus from their present fear to the eternal God, to replace what they didn't know about the future with what they did know about Him. They had to put away childish things (being afraid of everything) and grow up in their faith and understanding (4)

The most precise way to please God, is to recognize our emptiness and to learn from our predecessors. As someone narrated clearly:"One of the chief purposes of our Divine religion is to teach man where to find this indispensable element of strength. The Divine Word, coming from the very Maker of man, who knows us completely, declares that "he who trusteth in his own heart is a fool." We have no spiritual strength in ourselves. Just as our bodies derive all their strength from the food we eat, and every oak draws its strength from the surrounding earth and air, so our souls obtain all spiritual power from a source outside of us. Psalmist David, whose native weaknesses were deplorably conspicuous, was only strong when in alliance with God. His declaration is, "The Lord is my strength." This is the only strength which the Bible recognizes. Who are the Bible heroes? Men of genius, wits, orators, philosophers? No. They are the Enoch who walked with God, the Joseph who conquered sensual temptation because God was with him, the Elijah who stood like a granite pillar against the tides of idolatry, and the Daniel who never quailed at the lion's roar. Daniel gives us the secret of his strength in his three-times-a-day interviews with God. The Lord fed his inner soul as the subterranean springs feed a well and keep it full during summer droughts. God's strength is "made perfect in our weakness." This means that the Divine power is most conspicuous when our weakness is the most thoroughly felt. We have got first to be emptied of all self-conceit and self-confidence. A bucket cannot hold air and water at the same time. As the water comes in the air must go out. The meaning of some hard trials is to get the accursed spirit of self out of our hearts. When we have been emptied of self-trust, we are in the condition to be filled with might in the inner man by the power of the Holy Spirit. When Isaiah felt that he was but a child, and an unclean one at that, he received the touch of celestial fire. Peter had immense confidence in Peter when he boasted of his own strength; but after pride had got its fall, Peter is endued with power from on high, and then the apostle who was frightened by a servant-girl could face a Sanhedrin. A Christian must not only realize his own utter feebleness, but he must give up what world rely on, and admit that "vain is the help of man." (5)

The element of mystery is the love of God. The old saints and mystics reveled in their experience of His love, but they also remembered that their God was a "consuming fire". A mystic is simply someone who believes that there is a real spiritual world behind the physical world that we see; and a Christian sees Jesus Christ as Lord of both the seen and the unseen. God deliberately keeps some things secret so that you and I will stay humble and learn to trust Him even where we do not understand what He is doing. Before we try to tie all of this together, I hope and wish that you have the fear of the Lord.

If God is good and loving (and He is), and if God is all-powerful (and He is), and if God has a purpose and a plan that include His children (and He does), and if we are His children (as I hope you are), then there is no reason to fear anything, for God is in control of everything. (6)

Illustration:

'In all our lives, even the saddest and loneliest, there are sources of comfort and joy which have been prepared in the providence of God, but we are too much occupied with ourselves and our circumstances to behold them until God opens our eyes. Therefore, the Apostle says: "Eye hath not seen, nor ear heard, neither hath it entered into the heart of man, the things which God hath prepared for them that love him, but God hath revealed them unto us by His Spirit." We need the cleansed vision of faith; beside us stands our Lord with raiment for our rags, eye-salve for our blindness, health for our poverty, food for our famishing soul, and water for our thirst. It is not necessary to pray that He should come; He is already beside us. We need only two things— first, the grace of vision that we may see; secondly, the grace of appropriation that we may take.' (7)

From generation to generation, we can count on God's faithfulness. God in His infinite mercy has given us an unbreakable promise. His mercy endures forever. Human relationships come and go, but while our relationships may change, let's celebrate His unchanging love. His love letter to you is an invitation to reconsider your worship service. As Paul advises us *"Therefore, I urge you, brothers and sisters, in view of God's mercy, to offer your bodies as a living sacrifice, holy and pleasing to God--this is your true and proper worship.*

2 Do not conform to the pattern of this world, but be transformed by the renewing of your mind. Then you will be able to test and approve what God's will is--his good, pleasing and perfect will (Rom 12:1-2 NIV)

It is noteworthy to mention that "transformer" lives by power from within, but the "conformer" lives by pressure from without. To the believer who is transformed by God: " Let us come before God not defiled but cleansed in the blood of Christ, wearing His robe of righteousness, not sorrowful but rejoicing, not looking like slaves but as His children. One day Christians will be presented faultless before the Father's throne". (8)

As you read this book, my prayers are that you will grow in your conviction that

God is the answer to all your fears. God said "Call to me, and I will answer you; *I will tell you great things beyond the reach of your knowledge. (Jer 33:3 NAB.*

This scripture clearly tells us that if you do God's will, he will give you more than you asked for. This scripture gives us promises that will never end. God listens to all those who call unto him in truth. He will fulfill the desire of all man that fear him and he also hear their cry and he will save them. (9)

As you know very well, one of the chief characteristics of light is that it shows things, not as they might be, not as they are said to be, not as they ought to be, not as they are supposed to be, not as we would like them to be, but as they are!

In some way, how do you respond or manifest your love toward God? When God made man in His own likeness, He made him thereby capable of love. The heart of God is the well-spring of love; *For the LORD is good and his love endures forever; his faithfulness continues through all generations. (Psa 100:5 NIV)*

Hold on to God's eternal promises and spend some time reading His love letter to you

VII

WHERE DO WE GO FROM HERE?

So when we look at all of this information, it gives new insight into understanding those long-term repetitive struggles we have. Nevertheless, the cycle that so many of us find ourselves in get you pointed in the right direction according to Micah 6:8 *"He has told you, O man, what is good; And what does the LORD require of you But to do justice, to love kindness, And to walk humbly with your God? (Mic 6:8 NAS)* the Lord God has told us what is right and what he demands: See that justice is done, let mercy be your first concern, and humbly obey your God". But as I mentioned previously loving God implies Godly living because: Jesus Christ never changes! He is the same yesterday, today, and forever. Heb. 13:8

Choosing comes from the core of who we are.

When we truly choose, we have no one to blame and nowhere to hide. Choosing thrills us. Choosing scares us. Choosing is central to personhood. Poet Archibald MacLeish has said, "What is freedom? Freedom is the right to choose: the right to create for oneself the alternatives of choice. Without the possibility of choice a man is not a man but a member, an instrument, a thing." (1)

Dr. Neil Warren has a wonderful exercise to develop your decision-making muscle ... One of the primary reasons for inauthenticity in our lives, Neil says, is that we do not exercise our God-given, God-powered ability to choose. We look to others for signals. We choose options that will please or placate or appease rather than doing the hard work of courageously and wisely owning our decisions before God. (2)

Choosing involves warfare. Whenever we choose to worship God, the adversary will oppose us. The character of our worship depends on the condition of our heart, " *But without faith it is impossible to please him, for anyone who approaches God must believe that he exists and that he rewards those who seek him. (Heb 11:6 NAB)*

A worshipping church must of necessity be a warring church, for true worship is spiritual warfare. It is interesting to note that through the history, especially with the people of Israel the spiritual battle was fought at the tabernacle, while the physical battle was waged in the field. That's why we find this exhortation very powerful: *Therefore, since we have so great a cloud of witnesses surrounding us, let us also lay aside every encumbrance, and the sin which so easily entangles us, and let us run with endurance the race that is set before us,*

2 fixing our eyes on Jesus, the author and perfecter of faith, who for the joy set before Him endured the cross, despising the shame, and has sat down at the right hand of the throne of God.

3For consider Him who has endured such hostility by sinners against Himself, so that you may not grow weary and lose heart. (Heb 12:1-3 NAS)

"A man by himself is in bad company" someone once wrote. We could just as well add, "a man in search of his identity is traveling the wrong road." You don't have to go very far along that road to notice how quickly the landscape becomes flat, parched, and unpromising. The more you find out about yourself the more you realize how very insufficient it is. (3)

From the first chapter of Genesis we are taught more clearly than any words can teach us what man becomes when he is a center to himself and supposes that all things are revolving around him. The Bible records were given to us to take away the veil which hung between heaven and earth, between man and God. The actual revelation which has been made to us is of God in His relation to the soul of man. The self-declared object of the Scriptures is that men should know God and know themselves.

We need to cast ourselves into God's capable hands and depend on His love. He is the One who fills our lives with music. Difficulties need not break us; they can increase our love for life and bring us closer to God.

The LORD will command His lovingkindness in the daytime; And His song will be with me in the night, A prayer to the God of my life. (Psa 42:8 NAS)

The truth is, God formulated a perfect plan for every single person born since Adam. He only waits for each person to find out what that plan is and then to choose to walk in it. " God conceived a wonderful plan for every one of us. In His plan, we were predestined to become His sons and daughters at the Cross. But one potential obstacle stands between us and God's perfectly conceived purposes: Using the free will God has given us, we must choose to walk in the plan He has ordained for our lives. God looks for a way to approach each of us in order to present His personal plan for our lives. He begins with the preaching of the Cross that encourages us to accept Jesus Christ as Savior and Lord. If we accept Jesus, we take our first step into the plan God predestined for us before the foundations of the world. But if we reject Him, then like so many before us, we will live and die without ever taking that first step" (4)

Biblical teaching gives a very important place to the mind and the choices that it makes. Our mind has been given to us by God and he expects it to be used. But choice leads to action. Peter wrote *As a result, they do not live the rest of their earthly lives for evil human desires, but rather for the will of God. (1Pe 4:2 NIV).*

It is in the converse of mind with mind and spirit with spirit that we are conscious of our keenest interests and our most satisfying enjoyments. Man is spirit. This it is which makes him capable of intercourse and communion with God Himself. This it is which makes prayer possible, and thanksgiving possible, and worship possible, in more than a form and a name.

The choice to forgive becomes a commitment of your action and attitude in many areas. You choose never to repeat the wrong again to the person who hurt you, to a third party in the form of gossip, or to yourself (to the best of your ability) in the form of self-pity and righteous indignation. Forgiving is a big decision that should never be made lightly. (5)

Our daily communication with God implies forgiveness through prayer at the altar of our heart.— Only there can God meet with us. Only there can we meet with God. At the altar is reconciliation, and forgiveness, and peace; for the blood is there— the blood of the everlasting covenant. On that sacrificial blood we stand; round that altar we gather for worship and for fellowship. Standing there, we see the fire of heaven coming down, and the fire of the altar going up.

Such parabolic communication is needed to shock people out of their idolatrous liaisons through which they are becoming anaesthetized. The readers are to express their loyalty by means of being faithful witnesses to Christ, which necessitates no compromise with idolatry. John's strategy to move the readers to this ethical-theological goal is to address them through the medium of prophetic parabolic communication. (6)

To the question:

WHERE DO WE GO FROM HERE ?

Myself, yourself and the church all together have to deal generally with the issue of witnessing for Christ in the midst of a pagan culture, and express our loyalty by means of being faithful to the love of God which is the main point of this letter.

As a man thinks in his heart so is he." (Proverbs 23: 7)

Where you focus is key to your success. *"I call heaven and earth to witness against you today, that I have set before you life and death, the blessing and the curse. So choose life in order that you may live, you and your descendants, (Deu 30:19 NAS) "*.The negative and the positive of life are set before you. Focus on the negative and you will give life to it. Keep your eyes on the promise of God and you will give life to it. Which would you rather give life to? While it's ideal to turn away from your problem, what happens when your problem is right in your face and you have no choice but to stare it down every day? Henry David Thoreau said, "It's not what you look at that matters, it's what you see." I believe this to be true in cases where you have to face something that is unwanted. In those cases we should use the eyes of our faith. Don't let your mind linger on what you dislike but rather what you desire God to manifest. (7)

We live in a culture that primarily assesses someone's worth by what he or she accomplishes. We send out résumés that list our achievements. Even at parties we judge one another's productivity because the usual question upon meeting a stranger is "What do you do?"— as if by gathering such information we will really know who that individual is.

That societal attitude has probably invaded our own. One of the worst problems with which we struggle in our infirmities is that we are slowed down or even incapacitated by them. We develop an inferiority complex because we haven't fulfilled all of our goals or been as productive as someone else. When we get into such comparisons, we are really in trouble because we can always find someone who performs better than we. (8)

People with who prone to problems with anxiety and worry use their God-given gifts to scare themselves by over-thinking and over-reacting. They use their creativity to envision the worst-possible scenarios, most of which never happen. That may sound dramatic, but it's true. How precious is Thy lovingkindness, O God! And the children of men take refuge in the shadow of Thy wings. (Psa 36:7 NAS)

Let us acknowledge that this compulsion to pile up achievements is a mistaken response to the deepest hunger of our lives— a longing for God. No matter how much we produce, there will always be more things we could have done. We will never be satisfied, no matter how much we do. For as the early Church bishop and theologian Saint Augustine (354– 430) confessed, "Oh, Lord, thou hast made us, and our spirits are restless until we rest in thee." (9)

Psychiatrist and Christian leader John White addresses that problem at length in this excerpt from his powerful book on prayer:

It really does not matter how small we are, but how at peace we are with ourselves. And he is at peace who has seen himself appropriately placed in the total scheme of things. The problem is not that we are small but that we are competitive and therefore displaced persons in the mad scramble for a place in life. ...

To know that we are small yet accepted and loved, and that we fit into the exact niche in life a loving God has carved out for us is the most profoundly healthy thing I know. ... Most of all we are left free to wonder at the glory and majesty of God, drinking in drafts of living water and knowing what we are created for. (10)

And what we are created for is simply to wonder at God's exalted and gracious magnificence, to drink in the glories of His life in us, to wait in His presence with praise!

Praise is larger than gratitude, for praise is directed to God solely on the basis of who He is. Especially in times of disappointment, we can still praise the LORD for His character. We know that the Trinity is faithful, even when our prayers are not answered the way we would like. Praise arises from our trust that God is good, that His character of grace is unsurpassable. I know that I do not praise often and deeply enough, so I need training to cultivate the discipline. What about you? Shall we covenant together to increase praise in our lives? (11)

VIII

CARELESSNESS LEADS TO
A LOSS OF STANDARDS

Every government operates according to a set of values, that is the beliefs and moral commitments by which it makes policy and conducts its affairs. Ps.100 summarizes the way we should worship and serve the Lord.

> Shout praises to the Lord
> Everyone on this earth.
> Be joyful and sing
> As you come in
> To worship the Lord
> You know the Lord is God!
> He created us,
> And we belong to Him;
> We are His people,
> The sheep in his pasture
> Be thankful and praise the Lord
> As you enter his temple.
> The Lord is good!
> His love and faithfulness
> Will last forever.

Carelessness is often associated with a lapse in judgment or what are known as mind slips because the students had know-how to have avoided making the mistakes, but did not for undeterminable reasons.

In any education environment, careless mistakes are those errors that occur in areas within which the student has had training. Careless mistakes are common occurrences for students both within and outside of the learning environment. They are often associated with a lapse in judgment or what are known as mind slips because the students had know-how to have avoided making the mistakes, but did not for undeterminable reasons. Given that students that are competent of the subject and focused are most likely to make careless mistakes, concerns for students exhibiting careless mistakes often turn toward neurological disorders as the cause. (1)

Personal Bible study is the Christian's lifeline. It is never optional; it is always essential. When Paul urged his protégé Timothy, "Do your best to present yourselves to God as one approved, a workman who does not need to be ashamed and who correctly handles the word of truth" (2 Tim. 2: 15, NIV), he underscored the essential nature of the Scriptures in fostering high-quality spiritual living.

The Word of God is compared to a sword that is sharp and pierces people's consciences: *"For the word of God is alive and active. Sharper than any double-edged sword, it penetrates even to dividing soul and spirit, joints and marrow; it judges the thoughts and attitudes of the heart. (Heb 4:12 NIV)*.

In 1 Thessalonians 5: 4– 10 the "sons of the light" (Christians) are contrasted with "the sons of darkness" (unbelievers):

"But you, brothers, are not in darkness so that this day should surprise you like a thief. You are all sons of the light and sons of the day. We do not belong to the night or to the darkness. So then, let us not be like others, who are asleep, but let us be alert and self-controlled. For those who sleep, sleep at night, and those who get drunk, get drunk at night. But since we belong to the day, let us be self-controlled, putting on faith and love as a breastplate, and the hope of salvation as a helmet. For God did not appoint us to suffer wrath but to receive salvation through our Lord Jesus Christ. He died for us so that, whether we are awake or asleep, we may live together with him".

One area in which many Christians struggle is gratitude for grace. When we first come to Christ, every believer is on fire with thankfulness. But through the natural process of life, work, raising children, and whatever else may captivate your attention, it is easy to lose that deep sense of thankfulness. So believers feel strong because they have grown and hit a plateau on their walk. But there are no plateaus, only the constant, upward call of Christ Jesus. (2)

The greatest missing element in the consciousness of humanity is the goodness of God. Hebrews 4: 14-16 tells us we can pray boldly *Therefore, since we have a great high priest who has ascended into heaven, Jesus the Son of God, let us hold firmly to the faith we profess.*

15 *For we do not have a high priest who is unable to empathize with our weaknesses, but we have one who has been tempted in every way, just as we are--yet he did not sin.*

16 *Let us then approach God's throne of grace with confidence, so that we may receive mercy and find grace to help us in our time of need. (Heb 4:14-16 NIV)*–

Above all, pray with sincerity, honor, and humbleness before the Almighty God. "*Therefore confess your sins to each other and pray for each other so that you may be healed. The prayer of a righteous person is powerful and effective. (Jam 5:16 NIV).* (3)

What is prayer?

Prayer is so much more than a comforting exercise. Praying to God is talking to the creator of your very being. It is connecting with the God of the universe. You are invited to pray. God himself invites you to bring your burdens, your cares and your needs to him. He even invites you to come boldly in order to find mercy and grace to help in your times of need. He designed you to be in communication with Him.

Invited to pray

God cares about each one of us as individuals. The Bible tells us that he knows the number of hairs we each have on our head. He knows everyone who has ever wandered far from Him. You may feel sometimes like no one really knows who you are. God knows. He waits to hear your voice. You can pray because you are invited!

The prayer offered in faith, believing God hears and will answer, is prayer that brings power into our lives. Without faith nothing happens beyond the mere immediate comfort of prayer. Repetitious words are empty without faith. Believing God cares and is waiting to hear from you is the first step toward powerful prayer. God desires to heal the broken places in our lives. He tells us He will bring beauty out of the ashes we have made. He will bring joy where grieving has lived in our hearts. We pray because prayer is powerful and it moves God's heart.

God is waiting to connect with each one of us. Our natural selfishness and our willful and stubborn rebellion have created a disconnection with God. He wants to connect with us and work powerfully in our hearts and lives through prayer. (4)

Avoid to be careless about your spiritual gift(s)

Just as debris in a river can block the flow of the river, so the bondages in our life may block the flow of our God-given gifts. Bondage generally prevents our developing. Do not try to be someone other than yourself, be responsible. *But the one who does not know and does things deserving punishment will be beaten with few blows. From everyone who has been given much, much will be demanded; and from the one who has been entrusted with much, much more will be asked. (Luk 12:48 NIV)*

The Bible teaches that everybody who follows Jesus has received gifts from the Holy Spirit. Understanding and embracing the unique ways God has wired you is an indispensable part of discovering God's will for your life. Perhaps you are someone who loves to offer hospitality, or you are a born encourager, or administration comes naturally to you, or you have found yourself pursuing leadership activities since grade school. You have discovered a critical piece of God's road map for your life. Making decisions that are in line with the exercise of your spiritual gifts will honor God and bring you joy. (5)

Following God's will by faith

God comes to Noah. He says, "I want you to leave everything. I want you to build an ark. You're going to face ridicule and hostility. You're going to face judgment. You're going to face a decimated planet. You're going to face a flood, but I will be with you, Noah, and I'll give you a sign — a rainbow. Every time you see that rainbow, you'll know you're not alone."

Noah says, "Wow. I'll go." God comes to Abraham and says, "I want you to leave everything familiar — your home, your culture, your safety, your security, your language. I want you to go to a place I will show you, but I will be with you, and I will give you a sign that I will be with you. It's called circumcision." And Abraham says, "Noah got a rainbow. Couldn't it be, like, a secret handshake or a decoder ring or something like that?" God never says it's going to be easy, but sometimes people will deceive themselves that they are being "spiritual" when they are really doing anxiety management: "I just don't feel peace about it." When in the Bible does God ever tell someone like Moses, "Go to Pharaoh," or David, "Face Goliath," or Daniel, "Go into a lion's den," or Esther, "Face Haman," and have somebody say, "Yes, Lord. I feel peace about that"? Peace lies on the other side of obedience, on the other side of the door, not this side. Peace does not lie in getting God to give me other circumstances. Peace lies in finding God in these circumstances. (6).

Clearly, there is a high cost for *not sharing our faith:* there is an eternal consequence for those who have never heard. At the same time, there is a high cost *for sharing our faith as well!* The inevitable result of bold witness is persecution. While we simply cannot choose to remain silent, we cannot ignore the high cost of witness either.

Contextualization

It is axiomatic to point out that we cannot bring into existence what we do not already know and do ourselves. It is simply not possible to model what we have not yet experienced. As obvious as that sounds, this truth has profound implications when it comes to the significant role of worship in the cross-cultural enterprise. (7)

We often assume that we know exactly what God is doing. We tend to believe that we have a good understanding of both His methods and His purposes though it often turns out we are mistaken about both.

Paul Marshall is helpful at this point. First, he points out that the word Christian can be used in a variety of ways. It is not always easy to differentiate between the various definitions, but the categories that Marshall proposes are extremely helpful. He considered five types of Christian

1) Census Christians :are people who, if asked about their religion, would say, "Christian." This designation might not relate at all to anything that these people believe or practice. Often, this is a cultural answer. If asked about their religion in certain geographic areas, for example, many people might answer, "Of course I'm a Christian. Isn't everybody?" These people, according to Marshall, are "census Christians." On a census, these people would check the "Christian" box. What that designation actually means is anybody's guess.

2) Member Christians: claim some sort of identification with a particular Christian institution or organization. Again, this does not mean that these people necessarily participate or even that they show up at their church. These people simply have some sort of personal connection with a church and they identify themselves with that church. They might say, "I am Catholic," or "I am Baptist," or "I am Methodist."

3) *Practicing Christians:* actually participate in the life of a church. They typically attend worship services. In some fashion, these people are involved in the forms and rituals of the faith. Often their connection with the church is limited to weddings, baptisms, and funerals.

4) Believers (or Committed Believers): are people for whom the Christian faith is central and shaping. These Christians strive to live out their faith and communicate their faith to others. To use the language of the evangelical world, these people have a personal relationship with Jesus. Often they will use the language of John 3 and talk about being "born again."

5) Hidden Christians: are people who believe secretly. Fearful of persecution, these people keep their faith to themselves. In some settings, these believers might keep their faith secret from government officials and employers. In other settings, they might keep their faith secret from even family members and friends. These believers might not even experience specific acts of outward persecution, but the fear of persecution has caused their faith to be completely inward. For the most part, their faith, though real, is hidden. In most cases, they have not "joined" a church, though

this might be an artificial measurement since, in many settings, there is no official institutional church to join. (8)

PIVOT: the arrangement of subject matter so that there are pivotal points at which the story emphasizes our identity and our relationship; pivots act like hinges in the text.

In Ps 100
He created us,
And we belong to Him;
We are His people,
The sheep in his pasture
Be thankful and praise the Lord
As you enter his temple.

A brief look at the formation and preservation of the Bible throughout history reveals the high priority God has placed on ensuring that His revelation reaches men and women from generation to generation.

IX

THE TRUE MOTIVE OF ALL WORSHIP AND SERVICE IS MISSING.

Worship the LORD with gladness; come before him with joyful songs.3 Know that the LORD is God. It is he who made us, and we are his; we are his people, the sheep of his pasture. (Psa 100:2-3 NIV)

What Is Worship?

We struggle for words to describe worship of our all-powerful, all-sufficient, all-knowing, ever-present God. After all, He alone is Omnipotent, Omniscient, and Omnipresent. It is impossible to express sufficiently our love, reverence, respect, devotion, adulation, adoration, and veneration of the Ancient of Days. We struggle to find adequate words because the God we worship is beyond our comprehension. We need to be reminded that unless we seek him with all our hearts, our worship will be only empty service. The more we understand about God, the more we want to worship him. In the process, God reveals more of himself to us. He has done this through the ages.

Jesus' statement is the best definition of worship. Our Lord called his definition the greatest commandment: *"Love the Lord your God with all your heart and with all your soul and with all your mind and with all your strength.' (Mar 12:30 NIV.)*

Saying that worship has changed throughout human history is stating an obvious fact. Across cultures and belief systems, the worship of God and his son, Jesus Christ, has taken on many forms and expressions. This is true, despite the progress, at least that's what we call it, that our churches have made in their worship expression. We have more music, more energy, more expression, and more hands in the air— and all the while our impact on this culture gets smaller and smaller. We have seen worship, but have we seen revival?

King David. Long considered one of the greatest examples of worship, David had a unique and powerful relationship with God. In fact, God commended him for being a "man after my own heart." David was famous for his focused, unrestrained worship of the Lord, and he organized a system of worship for the entire Jewish nation to follow. David led his people as a worshipper of the Most High God. He wrote most of the Book of Psalms. Even during the time when seeking God's forgiveness for murder and adultery, David declared: "Lord, let me speak so I may praise you, the sacrifice God wants is a broken spirit .(1)

Moses introduced the tabernacle as the dwelling place of God. King David instituted worship structure. Solomon, his son, built a temple in which all the nations of the world could know Yahweh. Worship in the tabernacle and in the temple was highly organized and included a complex system of rituals, sacrifices, and feast. Worship was led exclusively by priests, and the musicians assisting in worship were part of the tribe of Levi.(2)

Worship in the Psalms

What can we learn about worship from the psalms?

1. **The psalms teach us to worship reverently in God's presence**. Reverence is an attitude of the heart, not necessarily reflected by the volume of our words or the movement of our feet.
2. **The psalms teach us to worship God with praise**. More than twenty psalms offer praise for all God has done in creation, sustaining our lives, saving us, and protecting us.
3. **Many psalms teach us to achieve intimacy with God through worship.**

   My soul yearns, even faints, for the courts of the LORD; my heart and my flesh cry out for the living God. (Psa 84:2 NIV)

   Better is one day in your courts than a thousand elsewhere; I would rather be a doorkeeper in the house of my God than dwell in the tents of the wicked. (Psa 84:10 NIV)

4. **Many psalms teach us to delight in worshipping God**.

   Whoever dwells in the shelter of the Most High will rest in the shadow of the Almighty. (Psa 91:1 NIV)

5. **The psalms teach us to express great love and appreciation in worship.**

   In Psalm 119, each verse expresses gratitude for the Word of God that gives guidance in life. For through the Word of God, people find joy, holiness, and direction for their lives.

6. **The psalms teach us to express faith in divine providence as we worship God**.

   The psalmist expresses great faith in God's guidance, protection, and providence. In Psalms 65 and 121, the psalmist expresses gratitude to God for his continued care.

7. **The psalms help the worshipper find refuge in God**. God is called a rock, a stronghold, and the One who protects his people. In Psalms 46, 61, and 62, the psalmist rejoices that God looks after him, protects him, and is the strength of his life.

8. **The psalms teach us to conquer our foes through worship**.

   For who is God besides the LORD? And who is the Rock except our God? (Psa 18:31 NIV)

9. **The psalms teach us to confess our sins in worship and ask for God's forgiveness.**

   Models of confession are found in Psalms 32, 78, 95, and 106.

10. **The psalms teach us to have passion in worship.**

    (Psa 42:1 As the deer pants for streams of water, so my soul pants for you, my God. 2 My soul thirsts for God, for the living God. When can I go and meet with God? (Psa 42 1-2 NIV)

11. **The psalms instruct us to sing praise to the name of the Lord (Ps 7: 17).**

12. **The psalms instruct us to make music skillfully and on a variety of instruments (Psalms 33; 150).**(3)

Jesus is the supreme worship leader through whom the new covenant is established. With the new covenant comes a change in our focus. All our worship is now focused on one person, Jesus. All the traditions, practices, prayers, sacrifices, and songs in the Old Testament point to Jesus. Followers of Christ can now worship God everywhere— in the streets, in the synagogue, on mountaintops, in caves, in homes and small buildings, and in prison. Most importantly, they can now worship Jesus in their hearts. Worship involves presenting our bodies to God as living sacrifices. These sacrifices are freely given and involve love and devotion to God. Worship is no longer defined by specific form or ritual, but by a much more personal element— spiritual gifts. Worship should become a part of our daily lifestyle. Early Christians were encouraged to present their bodies as living sacrifices to God in worship through Christian service, caring for their brothers and sisters in the Lord, and expressing their talents and gifts in private and public worship. The tone should be one of delight, joy, wonder, thanksgiving, and gratefulness. Jesus demanded willing service rather than mere outward conformity.

However, many practices in evangelical churches as people have been persuaded that they should express much of their worship via music and instrumentation, even through dance, other bodily movements and drama.

There is personal-pleasure worship, which puts the worshipper's enjoyment in first place, rather than God's desire. There is worldly-idiom worship, which borrows the current entertainment music of the world with its rhythms, instruments, actions and showbiz presentation, heedless of all the Bible's warnings about loving the world.

How is it that evangelicals have tumbled into this dramatic change of viewpoint?

What's causing good people to lose sight of a clear-cut definition of spiritual worship?

Here is as example the heart of the matter: …

Lights go down, the atmosphere changes, and the music starts. We are ready to worship.

The sound is loud, more gospel-ish, a bit funky, with enthusiastic trills from the worship director and solos from the choir. The choir sways, the rhythm is deep and steady, as the worship director both plays and directs, bringing the choir on the stage and the congregation on the floor together in song. Everyone around me is soon on their feet, clapping, singing, guided by words displayed on big screens overhead. As the first song fades, other musicians emerge on stage. Following a shift of finger-play on the piano, the new instruments strike a Latin beat or (Compas, Salsa and so on). Electric guitar, acoustic drums, and conga drums weave into the new song. People begin to whoop and yell both on and off stage. Both the choir and the crowd bounce up and down, keeping pace with a faster rhythm as the worship director smiles with affirmation. Then, another transition—a quieter song this time—and the bright lights on the platform focus on the piano playing a smooth melody with a contemporary beat I know is popular in many evangelical churches. The leader finishes the song with a quiet grace. The first worship set is over, and the teaching pastor for the night jumps into the spotlight to continue the service. (4)

By definition, to be profane is to treat sacred and biblical things with irreverence or disregard, so as to violate and pollute them.

This is simply profanity: profanity because it treats moral and sacred things with utmost irreverence and disregard. It actively and militantly decries biblical morality, substituting the opposite. It blatantly and vigorously promotes an alternative society, including the worship of self and of lust as normal, reasonable and acceptable, and that is its undisputed standing in the mind of the public.

For this reason the new worship movement is immensely wrong, and sins against God when it borrows and employs all the distinctive components of today's popular entertainment culture. Modern worship is a total artistic identification with that culture, contrary to the exhortation of 1 John 2.15-16: 'Love not the world, neither the things that are in the world. If any man love the world, the love of the Father is not in him. For all that is in the world, the lust of the flesh, and the lust of the eyes, and the pride of life, is not of the Father, but is of the world.'(5)

This is carnal, cynical, artificial and manipulative … It is undeniable that the new worship sets out to stir emotions externally and artificially.

Emotions fanned into flames by sentimental or stirring music may be enjoyable feelings at a purely human level, but they are not worship. The same goes for all artificially generated feelings. If a preacher moves people to weeping by telling 'tear-jerkers', their sense of need for God or their repentance will be nothing more than short-lived emotionalism. If, however, the people understand their need through hearing the Word (which is surely moving enough), their conviction and repentance will be genuine and lasting.

Music cannot really move the soul. It only moves the emotions. Valid worship starts in the mind. If it bypasses the understanding, it is not true worship. If it is overwhelmed by physical things, such as the skilful and moving performance of orchestras, it is compromised and spoiled. Such worship reminds us of the Israelites who wanted to supplement manna with other foods. Today many say to God (in effect): 'You are not enough; I need unusually loud or rhythmic music in addition, to excite me.' … Paul states the prime role of worship in these words: 'Let all things be done unto edifying' *What then shall we say, brothers and sisters? When you come together, each of you has a hymn, or a word of instruction, a revelation, a tongue or an interpretation. Everything must be done so that the church may be built up". (1Co 14:26 NIV)* The word edifying refers literally to the construction of a building, but Paul always uses it to mean the building up of the understanding. Every element of worship must be understood in order to be valid. We are spiritually moved, not by melody, beauty or spectacle, but by what we understand.(6)

. **John Wesley** in his advice to hymn singers written in 1781. He wrote: 'Above all sing spiritually. Have an eye to God in every word you sing. Aim at pleasing Him more than yourself or any other creature. Attend strictly to the sense of what you sing, AND SEE THAT YOUR HEART IS NOT CARRIED AWAY WITH THE SOUND, but offered to God continually; so shall your singing be such as the Lord will approve of here, and reward when He cometh in the clouds of Heaven.'(7).

This is the problem of pluralism. ***Pluralism is a philosophy*** that allows for a wide diversity of viewpoints and doctrines to co-exist within a single body. Because so many doctrinal disputes have emerged within some churches, they have tried to keep the peace and unity, and at the same time accommodate differing views within the church. It is an attempt to accommodate conflicting viewpoints.

As the church becomes more pluralistic, the number of contradictory viewpoints that are tolerated increases. In turn, organizational and structural unity become the central concern. People strive to keep the church visibly united at all costs. However, there is always a price tag for that, and historically, the price tag has been the confessional purity of the churches.

When the Protestant movement began in the sixteenth and seventeenth centuries, confessions were created. These were creedal statements that set forth the doctrines that were embraced and confessed by these particular churches. For the most part, these confessional documents summarize the core tenets of what it means to be a Christian— things such as a belief in the Trinity, Christ as one person with two natures, and the bodily resurrection.

For centuries, Protestantism was defined by the body of doctrine that was confessed by each organization. But in our day, part of the impact of the ecumenical movement has been the relativizing of these older confessions. (8)

A striking resemblance to what some Churches today are allowing to creep in through Psychology and the Human Potential Movement, like offerings that appeal to the pride of life, the lust of the eye, and the lusts of the flesh . . . things offered on the altar of success for the sake of favor with the "world". (9)

Revelation 2:1-7 pictures the Ephesians' congregation as one credited with works, toil and patience, one that has rejected false apostles, and one that hated the work of the Nicolaitans. However its fault was that it had lost its first love, its original zealousness for the Lord and His coming. This seems to harmonize well with the history of the first century Church whose original zeal and ardor is the model for all succeeding time, (Acts 1-28). The loss of this original fire by the time that John wrote AD 95-96 can hardly be disputed. The "Nicolaitans" (Νικολαϊτῶν)Nikolaiton, vs.6)-derived from Nikao, to conquer, and laos, people-refers to "laity-conquerors," the hating of these sees the early Church's resistance to an Episcopal hierarchy and priestly caste as long as the apostles survived. The rejection of false apostles would correspond to the fact that generally the early Gnostic and anti-Trinitarian heresies, although started often in the first century, did not gain sweeping footholds across the land until the second and third centuries *"For such men are false apostles, deceitful workers, disguising themselves as apostles of Christ." (2Co 11:13 NAS)* The

Judaizing heresy was resisted in the first century, and then, as the face of Christendom turned more Gentile, it vanished (Acts 15; Gal 1-6). (10)

"But I have this against you, that you have left your first love. (Rev 2:4 NAS).

What a shock to be told that you don't love Christ as you once did. Love should grow, not wither. One commentator wrote: "To have something against friend or brother may be very human . . . But when it is the Lord who has something against the Church, it is time to tremble; and when that thing is loss of love, the Church should not only tremble, it should fall on its knees. Jesus warned the Church at Ephesus that it would lose its light and its testimony in the community, if the first love was not revived *"'Remember therefore from where you have fallen, and repent and do the deeds you did at first; or else I am coming to you, and will remove your lampstand out of its place-- unless you repent.*

(Rev 2:5 NAS). This actually happened many years later when Ephesus declined as a city. It is now uninhabited and one of the major ruins of the area. What a warning this is to Churches that have lost their first love. Looking at the outside, the Church at Ephesus appeared to be a model Church. However, inside the love was growing cold; the people were involved in their "good works" out of a sense of duty. The historical era of this Church was A.D. 33-100. Christ ends every one of His letters to the Churches with the same conclusion: *"'He who has an ear, let him hear what the Spirit says to the churches. To him who overcomes, I will grant to eat of the tree of life, which is in the Paradise of God.' (Rev 2:7 NAS).* (11)

The Ephesian Church was still, as it had been from the beginning, guarding the way, testing all new teachers, and rejecting with sure judgment the unworthy.

Every letter is to be understood as addressed partly to the Christians of the city, but still more to the true Christians of the entire Church. The idea that the individual Church is part of the Universal Church, that it stands for it after the usual symbolic fashion of the Apocalypse, is never far from the writer's mind; and he passes rapidly between the two points of view, the direct address to the local Church as an individual body with special needs of its own, and the general application and apostrophe to the entire Church as symbolized by the particular local Church. (12)

True worship has always been a matter of the heart. We again urge readers to consider this central principle of worship, because how we worship is not just a matter of culture or taste or generation, but a matter of God-given rules. Principles count.

The Lord requires that we worship Him 'in spirit and in truth'. The 'truth' part of this means that worship must be right, and also that it must be understandable or rational.

X

THE LOVE THAT DEFINES US

This complaint drives me to take the time to address the deepest insecurities that all of us possess. I also want to answer this question and share a sincere truth with you about how our Father in heaven feels about us. A possible avenue is to use the seven churches to foreshadow seven different periods in the history of the Church. The problem with this view is that each of the seven churches describes issues that could fit the Church in any time in its history. So, although there may be some truth to the seven churches representing seven eras, there is far too much speculation in this regard. My focus would be on what message God is giving us through the seven churches, specially, the church that had forsaken its first love (2:4)

Notice the words "I know." These are very encouraging words. Jesus knows what you have done for Him. He has not overlooked your hard work or your sufferings on His account. Jesus points to 7 positive things in their church.

1. Their deeds = good works
2. Their toil = hard work
3. Their perseverance = endurance
4. They could not endure evil men = intolerance of false teachers
5. They had discernment = They "put to the test"
6. They had not grown weary = They refused to give up
7. They hated the deeds of the Nicolaitans = They opposed the cults. (1)

"The One who holds the seven stars in His right hand"

In holding the seven stars Jesus shows His role as protector of the church. He is also the owner of the churches. They are in His right hand. "the One who walks among the seven golden lampstands" The lampstands are the churches (1:20). *"As for the mystery of the seven stars which you saw in My right hand, and the seven golden lampstands: the seven stars are the angels of the seven churches, and the seven lampstands are the seven churches. (Rev 1:20 NAS)*Jesus walks among His churches. It is His responsibility to inspect the lamps and do what is necessary to keep them burning. He is the Lord of the churches and the Judge of the churches. We are accountable to Him. He is active, not passive in His responsibility. He is walking, not sitting or standing. (2)

There is so much to learn and to benefit from John's letter to the church at Ephesus, surely God wants us to pay attention to his warnings in order to realign our lives according to His will as a result of his love.

God speaks in a number of ways.

The first and most reliable way he speaks is through his word. The Bible is the manual for life and the measuring stick for all other forms of his communication. If you want to know God's will for your life, you'll want to know the kind of person he wants you to be, the kind of life he wants you to live, and the goals he wants you to achieve. Simple fact: if you want to know God's will, you need to get in God's word. Also, it's important to remember that God never contradicts his word. Everything that you think God might be saying to you should lineup with what he has already revealed in the Bible. God also speaks in more subtle ways through the Holy Spirit. (3).

Apostle Paul's ultimate goal in life, expressed so well in Phil.3:10 *That I may know him, and the power of his resurrection, and the fellowship of his sufferings, being made conformable unto his death; (Phi 3:10 KJV)*

I have loved thee with an everlasting love' (Jer. 31: 3),

Perhaps the lesson here flows directly from the heart of God. In his infinite love for us, God doesn't want us merely to have better information about Him, but to know Him. This is the story of how the God of Israel moves and works through the ages to make his will, love and purposes known. In one sense, this is a documentation of God's work for each generation as he makes himself known to man.

A love which rejoiced over the most unworthy objects, over lost ones recovered even from the depths of the vice and iniquity which made Rome, in the language of its own historians, 'the common sink and sewer' of the world. (4)

Most Christians in the early church came from society's underprivileged class, the dispossessed, slaves and outcasts. Thus, some nonbelievers attacked Christianity as a movement of the uneducated and powerless, set on undermining the Roman Empire. Celsus, for instance, declared that it had "its chief hold among the ignorant". To the contrary, though, Christianity was not based on ignorance. Rather, those who became Christians were committed to learning and advancement. The teaching of Christianity supported the government. As Christians gained education, they also gained social prominence. Highly conflict has emerged from different perceptions and lifestyles and the distinction was clearly observed in the society.

Rome, the mistress of the world, the mightiest city perhaps the world had ever seen, where, side by side, were found splendor and squalor, philosophy and filth, moral corruption and material magnificence, savage cruelty and effeminate luxury. (5)

The question, '**Who am I?**' which seems so pressing when we are young is not really the crucial question to ask. After all, as Mr. Keyes makes clear, our true identity is hidden in God and won't be revealed until we are with God. We are not, right now, in a position to appreciate or even guess at our real potential. In the meantime a better question to ask is, 'What must I do to do God's will?' That is the part we should play. The cultivation of ourselves is a business better left to God. He will do an enormously better job at it than we will. (6)

In Jeremiah 31: 3, .*The LORD appeared to us in the past, saying: "I have loved you with an everlasting love; I have drawn you with unfailing kindness. (Jer 31:3 NIV)* .

We cannot estimate the length of God's love. When did it begin to be? Long before I was born. Long before the Cross was raised on the brow of

Calvary. Long before the world was made. Its foundations lie in His own eternity. When we think on what He has done, and how God loved the world, we may be quite sure that He has loved us; sure also that He Who has loved us, and washed us from our sins in His own blood, will love us unto the end, and will keep us as the apple of His eye.

That is also the way that God feels about you. He loves you with an everlasting love, and with lovingkindness He has attempted to draw you toward Himself. If you have been resisting, please stop. It is time to enter into the joy, confidence, and security that await the children of God who understand the fullness of His love for them. (7)

Confidence in His love

He has His own plans for us all. He knows exactly what we want, and what is really best for each of us, and He never makes a mistake in planning for our good.

Love given and received is vital to our sense of self. Modern psychology has told us of our need to be loved. The biblical writers say this as well, but put the emphasis also on our need to love. If we do not love we are very much less than we were made to be. If we do love, our sense of identity grows. (8)

There is also a 'love problem' with our models. To love as Jesus taught, we must fly in the face of many of our modern hero-systems. Many of today's models are heroic because they live without commitment, obligation, responsibility or even emotional involvement. They are heroic for exploiting others sexually, psychologically, and financially. They are heroic precisely because of these lapses; their appeal is in the power that is gained through exploitation.

By modern standards, biblical love seems very unheroic and dull. To love with your whole heart you must have your own hero-system that is closer to the models of the Bible. Otherwise you will be pulled in two directions at once toward Christian love on the one hand, and to the attractiveness of power-through-exploitation on the other. Christian love demands sustained commitment; this requires a certain level of dominion over ourselves. (9)

In summary, let us remember that humankind as the image of God has an identity rooted in and derived from the Creator. Our struggle for identity in all its breadth can thus be best understood in terms of the character of God and of our interaction with him. Our identity comes from a source beyond itself. It is an identity derived.

No matter how spectacular, gifted, or dedicated a person might be, without love it is all ashes at God's feet. The subtraction of love is the great subtraction. No matter how much else I have or do, it comes to nothing without love. It is much like multiplying by zero in mathematics. No matter how large a number we multiply by zero, the result is always the same - zero.

Paul points out three things that are true of the person who does not love: 'I am nothing,' 'I gain nothing,' 'I just make noise.' This is a vivid picture of a shattered identity. Neither nihilist literature nor the theatre of the absurd says anything more degrading about human beings than Paul has said about those who have no love. They are nothing, they achieve nothing, they are without purpose or meaning. They are just a loud nuisance. (10)

So faith, hope, love remain, these three; but the greatest of these is love. (1Co 13:13 NAB)

What ultimately matters in life is not one's power, possession or position, but one's attitude and response to God:

O taste and see that the LORD is good;
How blessed is the man who takes refuge in Him!
O fear the LORD, you His saints;

For to those who fear Him, there is no want.
(Psa 34:8-9 NAS)

When we take that first step of obedience in following God, we will discover that he is good and kind. When we begin the Christian life, our knowledge of God is partial and incomplete. As we trust him daily, we experience how good he is.

Each church has its own personality, and peculiarities. Each church of today can find characteristics of itself both positive and negative in these seven churches. Each church has some areas to be praised and some areas to be improved.

Up to this point our study has centered around explanations of various biblical passages pertaining to the theme of this book. For the most part, there has been no direct attempt to explain how the biblical notion of people reflecting the images to which they are committed is relevant to or expressed in our contemporary world. Part of the reason for this is that there have been quite a few books attempting to explore how the biblical notion of idolatry is expressed in the contemporary world; part of the reason also is, this text precisely centered on the issue of Godly discontentment which is a complaint and an dissatisfaction

Nevertheless, the concluding chapter explores this particular letter as a mirror in which you can see yourself and your church and an invitation from the one who holds the seven stars in his right hand saying to you and me:" Think about where you are fallen from, and then turn back and do as you did at first.

If you reach that point, you can realize that this book contains a brief study on a very important but neglected subject, that is, the subject of ***repentance***

We will see that God does not exclude anyone in His invitation; however, sinners do exclude themselves. Listen to these lines from Philip Bliss's hymn

"Whosoever Will":

"Whosoever heareth," shout, shout the sound! Spread the blessed tidings all the world around;

Tell the joyful news wherever man is found,

"Whosoever will may come."

Whosoever cometh need not delay,

Now the door is open, enter while you may;

Jesus is the true, the only Living Way:

"Whosoever will may come."

"Whosoever will," the promise is secure;

"Whosoever will," forever must endure;

"Whosoever will!" 'tis life forever more;

"Whosoever will may come."

"Whosoever will, whosoever will!"

Send the proclamation over vale and hill

'Tis a loving Father calls the wanderer home:

"Whosoever will may come." (11)

Everything we have told you about (rejection, abandonment) has already happened in God's Word. God's people have been experiencing these things for a long time, and God has been taking care of His people for a long time.

Let's conclude this reading, the way that I started:

"Go and proclaim in the ears of Jerusalem, saying, " Thus says the Lord, I remember concerning you the devotion of your youth, the love of your betrothals, your following after Me in the wilderness, through a land not sown (Jer.2:2}NAS

Take care, brothers, lest there be in any of you an evil, unbelieving heart, leading you to fall away from the living God. But exhort one another every day, as long as it is called "today," that none of you may be hardened by the deceitfulness of sin. For we have come to share in Christ, if indeed we hold our original confidence firm to the end. Hebrews 3: 12– 14

XI

PRAISE & CELEBRATION

1 Listen, you heavens, and I will speak;
hear, you earth, the words of my mouth.

2 Let my teaching fall like rain and my words descend like dew,
like showers on new grass, like abundant rain on tender plants.

3 I will proclaim the name of the LORD.
Oh, praise the greatness of our God!

4 He is the Rock, his works are perfect, and all his ways are just.
A faithful God who does no wrong, upright and just is he.

Deuteronomy 32:1-4(NIV)

Reverence is sensitivity to God's presence and awareness of his intimate
fellowship with us

> O for a thousand tongues to sing
> Glory to God, and praise and love
> Be ever, ever given,
> By saints below and saints above,
> The church in earth and heaven

II

On this glad day the glorious Sun
Of righteous arose,
On my benighted soul he shone
And filled it with repose.

III

O for a thousand tongues to sing
My great Redeemer's praise!
The glory of my God and King,
The triumphs of his grace.

IV

My gracious Master and my God,
Assist me to proclaim,
To spread through all the earth abroad
The honors of thy name
Charles Wesley

In recent days, God is again stirring hearts to worship Him in spirit and in truth." *For God has not given us a spirit of timidity, but of power and love and discipline. (2Ti 1:7 NAS)*

I wrote this book because I perceive shame and fear as a real and present danger in the body of Christ. Many Christians are not living lives free of shame and fear,. Like many others, they felt embarrassed to be identified as a follower of Christ. Jesus demanded willing worship rather than mere outward conformity. Your coworkers or other associates may even think you're ashamed of your faith if you avoid talking about it or hide your true thoughts and feelings. Apostle Paul felt no shame at the message of Christ because he saw that it was powerful enough to transform lives. *For I am not ashamed of the gospel, because it is the power of God that brings salvation to everyone who believes: first to the Jew, then to the Gentile. (Rom 1:16 NIV)*

The most devout king David danced with all his might before the Ark of God, calling to mind the benefits granted to his forefathers in days past. So are we invited to praise and celebrate our heavenly Father.

Don't forget, the Bible says that natural people can't understand the things of God. It's to be expected that people who are walking in the power of the Holy Spirit will be misunderstood. If people mock or misjudge us because of an active relationship with God in the Spirit, it won't be the first time. It's a good opportunity to ask ourselves if we're more concerned with what people think of us than we are with growing in intimacy with God. *If you are insulted because of the name of Christ, you are blessed, for the Spirit of glory and of God rests on you. (1Pe 4:14 NIV)* .(1)

Besides offering praise to God in the congregation, we should never be shamed to proclaim to friends and companions "what God has done for us."

My biblical knowledge, leadership position, seminary training, experience, and skills all totally dedicated to honoring my Savior. St. Teresa of Avila wrote in The Way of Perfection: "Almost all problems in the spiritual life stem from a lack of self-knowledge."

John Calvin in 1530 wrote in his opening of his Institutes of the Christian Religion: "Our wisdom ... consists almost entirely of two parts: the knowledge of God and of ourselves. But as these are connected together by many ties, it is not easy to determine which of the two precedes and gives birth to the other."(2)

Ex. 15, "He is my God and I will glorify him; the God of my father, and I will exalt him;" Deut. 32, "Let my doctrine gather as the rain, let my speech distill as the dew;" Ps. 33, "I will bless the Lord at all times, his praise shall be always in my mouth."

These ornamental repetitions are of frequent occurrence among the prophets. The first part of the verse, then, conveys to us the happiness of the man who breaks not the law of God; but David making use of a metaphor, conveys the idea in a poetic manner.

Blessed is the one who does not walk in step with the wicked or stand in the way that sinners take or sit in the company of mockers, (Psa 1:1 NIV)

"Happy," says he, "is the man who hath not walked," etc.; that is to say, happy is he who is really just: and he is just who hath not gone in the counsel of the ungodly; that is to say, who has not followed the counsel, laws, or opinion of the wicked, which are altogether at variance with the way, that is, the law of God. The second part of the same verse expresses the same in similar words. For, when he says, "Nor stood in the way of sinners," he does not mean standing but walking. Standing here does not mean simply to stand, but to walk, and to continue walking. "Who hath not walked in the counsel of the ungodly, nor stood in the way of sinners," are here synonymous, for both convey that he is just who retires from the way, that is, from the law and counsel of sinners. And as the law of God is broken not only by the evil doer but also by the evil teacher, according to Mt. 5, "Whosoever, therefore, shall break one of those least commandments, and shall teach men so, he shall be called the least in the kingdom of heaven;" the prophet, therefore, adds: "nor sat in the chair of pestilence;" as much as to say, Blessed is he who neither in word nor deed broke through the law of God. "To sit in the chair of pestilence" means, to be among, to keep company with wicked men, with them to despise the law of God, as in no wise pertaining to a happy life, but, on the contrary, looking upon it as more advantageous to indulge in all the passions and desires of the flesh. The words, "sitting in the chair of pestilence," are well expressed by Malach. 3, "You have said: He laboreth in vain that serveth God, and what profit is it that we have kept his ordinances?" (3)

Because this topic is of great importance for all of us,thus, the fact that we may be in very good spiritual shape today is not necessarily indicative of how we will be in a year, or two, or five or ten. If the Lord delays His coming then there is more opportunity to "grow in grace, and in the knowledge of our Lord and Saviour Jesus Christ" (2 Peter 3: 18).

There are people who after decades of fighting the Christian battle, are still here, faithful, strong, loving, obedient, for whom the day for Christ's return is very important— but not critical. What is critical is that they remain obedient and solid in the Faith and to God and Jesus Christ until the very end.(4)

A Christian's primary motive for obedience should be Love for God; it should be common sense — that is understanding that all God commandments are there for our good.

Gratitude should be another major motivator, as mentioned above.

Gratitude for what God and Jesus have done for us. *I Will bless the LORD at all times; His praise shall continually be in my mouth. (Psa 34:1 NAS)*

These motivators should come before fear; and yet, in all too many cases, these motivators have not been there and, thus, some people have fallen by the wayside ... (5)

What the Scriptures tell us is,

We are instructed to tell the nations of his glory; tell all people the miracles he does. Why? Because it is a command:

"Tell of His glory among the nations, His wonderful deeds among all the peoples.

For great is the LORD, and greatly to be praised; He is to be feared above all gods. (Psa 96:3-4 NAS)"

"If you don't want to stay on the straight and narrow motivated by love and common sense and gratitude then know that taking the way of God lightly; that taking Jesus Christ's sacrifice lightly, will lead to dire consequences."

It's a scary thought, but it's meant to be there to catch us as we fall, as a safety net catches an acrobat who is falling and would get killed if the net would not be there.(6)

The people whose love will grow cold will make the terrible mistake of turning the church into a social club, rather than a treatment center.

The Christian world is dotted with social clubs. They are called churches — and, perhaps, once they were churches. In time, though, congregations run the risk of becoming social clubs. They are no longer places where people heal spiritually; where they grow and become better and spiritually healthier Christians; they are instead places where there is an obsessive concern with which social activity will come next. The focus becomes socials, bingo nights, trips, dances, etc, which in and by themselves can be healthy and good for a healthy congregation that keeps its priorities straight

Some ministers will turn more and more to psychology for inspiration, or pop theology books and less and less on the Bible. The Christians whose love will wax cold will have little use for the Bible, and the result will be disastrous. (7)

Whether in formal or informal contexts, Christians praised and honored God through music and song. As one observer expressed it, "The Christian Church was born in song." Meanwhile, there is an informal worship, in which casual, jokey, trivia-injecting leaders turn churches into sitting rooms, so depriving the Lord of dignity, reverence, grandeur and glory.

Paul encouraged the Christians in Ephesus to *"speaking to one another in psalms and hymns and spiritual songs, singing and making melody with your heart to the Lord; (Eph 5:19 NAS).*

(Psa. 98: 1-3).— The sacred poet says that he has been inspired to sing because God has done marvelous things. The return from the Exile was a marvel, but far more marvelous is the life of Christ. It is an inexhaustible magazine of marvels. What wonder there is in the incarnation, in the teaching of Christ, in His miracles, in His character, in His death! Then the experience of every Christian is a marvel— a world of marvel. What wonder in the awakening of a soul, in conversion, in sanctification!

Although in nature and in providence there are innumerable reasons for praising God, the songs of redeemed souls will always be principally inspired by the work of salvation. God is glorious as Creator, but the name by which the saints always know Him is 'the God of salvation.'(8)

Someone said: when God measures a man, He puts the tape around the heart instead of the head," *The LORD does not look at the things people look at. People look at the outward appearance, but the LORD looks at the heart." (1Sa 16:7 NIV)*

Too many churchgoers are singing" Standing on the Promises" when all they are doing is sitting on the premises.

Author unknown

BIBLIOGRAPHY

Introduction

1   Pascal, Pensees, #43
    Keyes, Dick. Beyond Identity: Finding your 'self' in the image and character of God (Kindle Locations 32-35). Destinee Media. Kindle Edition
    MacArthur, John F.. Revelation (MacArthur Bible Studies) (Kindle Locations 342-347). Thomas Nelson. Kindle Edition.

Chapter # 1

1   Schmidt, Ken M.. "Not Afraid To Tell the Truth" : Exposing Apostasy and the Conspiracy of Silence in the last days! (Kindle Locations 20279-20283). Xlibris. Kindle Edition.
2   Ibid … (Kindle Locations 20311-20326). Xlibris. Kindle Edition.
3   Galatians by G. Walter Hansen p.180
4   Bill Johnson. God is Good: Free Feature Message (Kindle Locations 42-43). Destiny Image. Kindle Edition
5   Schmidt, Ken M.. "Not Afraid To Tell the Truth" : Exposing Apostasy and the Conspiracy of Silence in the last days! (Kindle Locations 344-349). Xlibris. Kindle Edition.
6   Cleveland, Christena. Disunity in Christ: Uncovering the Hidden Forces that Keep Us Apart (p. 127). InterVarsity Press. Kindle Edition.
7   Schmidt, Ken M.. "Not Afraid To Tell the Truth" : Exposing Apostasy and the Conspiracy of Silence in the last days! (Kindle Locations 18077-18079). Xlibris. Kindle Edition.
8   Schmidt, Ken M.. "Not Afraid To Tell the Truth" : Exposing Apostasy and the Conspiracy of Silence in the last days! (Kindle Locations 544-546). Xlibris. Kindle Edition.
9   Ibid …! (Kindle Locations 5118-5130). Xlibris. Kindle Edition.
10 Houge, Adam. Because He is Your Lord Worship Him (Kindle Locations 221-224). . Kindle Edition.

11 Cleveland, Christena. Disunity in Christ: Uncovering the Hidden Forces that Keep Us Apart (pp. 189-190). InterVarsity Press. Kindle Edition.

12 MacDonald, William. Believer's Bible Commentary (p. 985). Thomas Nelson. Kindle Edition.

Chapter #2

1 NKJV, The Charles F. Stanley Life Principles Bible, eBook (Kindle Locations 123129-123133). Thomas Nelson. Kindle Edition.

2 G. K. Beale. We Become What We Worship: A Biblical Theology of Idolatry (Kindle Locations 3224-3226). Kindle Edition.

3 NKJV, The Charles F. Stanley Life Principles Bible, eBook (Kindle Locations 122618-122628). Thomas Nelson. Kindle Edition.

4 Spencer, Kristin N.. You Aren't Worthless: Unlock the Truth to Godly Confidence (Kindle Locations 1521-1523). Sincerely Adorned Books. Kindle Edition.

5 Gary Thomas, Sacred Pathways (Nashville: Thomas Nelson,!982,) 16sa

6 Spencer, Kristin N.. You Aren't Worthless: Unlock the Truth to Godly Confidence (Kindle Locations 1326-1328). Sincerely Adorned Books. Kindle Edition.

7 Keyes, Dick. Beyond Identity: Finding your 'self' in the image and character of God (Kindle Locations 245-262). Destinee Media. Kindle Edition.

8 NKJV, The Charles F. Stanley Life Principles Bible, eBook (Kindle Locations 108544-108549). Thomas Nelson. Kindle Edition.

Chapter # 3

1 Arnold, Thomas; Maurice, F.D.; Burgon, John. Church Pulpit Commentary (12 vol. Now In One) (Kindle Locations 95117-95121). www.DelmarvaPublications.com. Kindle Edition.

2 Keyes, Dick. Beyond Identity: Finding your 'self' in the image and character of God (Kindle Locations 99-101). Destinee Media. Kindle Edition

3 Ortberg, John. What Is God's Will for My Life? (p. 13). Tyndale House Publishers, Inc.. Kindle Edition.

4 The Transforming Power of Prayer Colorado Springs :NavPress, 1996

5 Pope, Russ. Understanding Our Struggles (Kindle Locations 93-94). . Kindle Edition.

6 Ibid … (Kindle Locations 51-54). . Kindle Edition.

7 Ibid (Kindle Locations 67-70). . Kindle Edition

8 Ibid … (Kindle Locations 80-81). . Kindle Edition.

9 Spencer, Kristin N.. You Aren't Worthless: Unlock the Truth to Godly Confidence (Kindle Location 922-932). Sincerely Adorned Books. Kindle Edition.

10 Ibid ... (Kindle Locations 967-970). Sincerely Adorned Books. Kindle Edition.

11 Ibid ... (Kindle Locations 1492-1494). Sincerely Adorned Books. Kindle Edition.

12 Thomas sacred pathways, 16

13 Pope, Russ. Understanding Our Struggles (Kindle Locations 223-225). . Kindle Edition

14 Keyes, Dick. Beyond Identity: Finding your 'self' in the image and character of God (Kindle Location 1205). Destinee Media. Kindle Edition.

Chapter # 4

1 Paul Tournier, Guilt and Grace (San Francisco, Calif.: Harper and Row, 1958), 97

2 Sproul, R.C.. What Is Repentance? (Crucial Questions) (pp. 3-5). . Kindle Edition.

3 Ibid ... (Crucial Questions) (pp. 26-28). . Kindle Edition.

4 Smith, Uriah. Daniel and the Revelation (Kindle Location 5120). . Kindle Edition.

5 Scazzero, Peter; Scazzero, Peter. Emotionally Healthy Spirituality: It's Impossible to Be Spiritually Mature, While Remaining Emotionally Immature (p. 93). Zondervan. Kindle Edition

6 What's your God language p118-119 Tyndale House Publishers, inc

7 Arnold, Thomas; Maurice, F.D.; Burgon, John. Church Pulpit Commentary (12 vol. Now In One) (Kindle Locations 4831-4834). www.DelmarvaPublications.com. Kindle Edition.

8 G. K. Beale. We Become What We Worship: A Biblical Theology of Idolatry (Kindle Locations 3233-3248). Kindle Edition.

9 Sheed, Frank. Theology and Sanity (p. 3). Catholic Way Publishing. Kindle Edition.

10 Sproul, R.C.. What Is Repentance? (Crucial Questions) (p.30- 31). . Kindle Edition.

11 Schmidt, Ken M.. "Not Afraid To Tell the Truth" : Exposing Apostasy and the Conspiracy of Silence in the last days! (Kindle Locations 4541-4559). Xlibris. Kindle Edition.

12 Joy, Trevor; Shelton, Spence. The People of God: Empowering the Church to Make Disciples (pp. 120-121). B&H Publishing Group. Kindle Edition.

13 Carr, Kelly. Revelation: Book of Mystery and Majesty (p. 10). Franklin Publishing. Kindle Edition

Chapter # 5

1 Negro History and Literature and contributing editor FREEDOMWAYS magazine. AFRO-U.S.A. is an expanded and enlarged version of the prestigious Negro Almanac, first published in 1967 and now completely revised and updated for the 1070's

2 NKJV, The Charles F. Stanley Life Principles Bible, eBook (Kindle Locations 58233-58239). Thomas Nelson. Kindle Edition.

3 Berrey, Timothy W.. Planning Your Life God's Way: Practical Help from the Bible for Making Decisions (Kindle Locations 2000-2003). Kindle Edition.

4 Ibid ... (Kindle Locations 3017-3019). Kindle Edition.

5 Ibid ... (Kindle Locations 1923-1925). Kindle Edition.

6 Ibid ... (Kindle Locations 1953-1956). Kindle Edition.

7 Ibid ... (Kindle Locations 2000-2003). Kindle Edition.

8 Ibid ... (Kindle Locations 3017-3019). Kindle Edition.

9 Publishing Cuyler, Theodore. God's Light on Dark Clouds (Kindle Locations 244-249). GLH. Kindle Edition.

10 Davis, Lynn R. How God Sees Your Struggles: Encouraging Yourself, Finding Strength And Developing A Spiritual Perspective (p. 22). Lynn R Davis. Kindle Edition.

11 Ibid ... (p. 47). Lynn R Davis. Kindle Edition.

12 Ibid ... (p. 8). Lynn R Davis. Kindle Edition.

13 MacArthur Jr., John. Standing Strong: How to Resist the Enemy of Your Soul (John MacArthur Study) (Kindle Locations 1020-1026). David C. Cook. Kindle Edition

Chapter # 6

1 Ortberg, John. What Is God's Will for My Life? (pp. 72-73). Tyndale House Publishers, Inc.. Kindle Edition

2 Sam Whiting, "Muni Driver Will Make New Friends, Keep the Old," San Francisco Chronicle, September 8, 2013, http:// www.sfchronicle.com/ bayarea/ article/ Muni-driver-will-make-new-friends-keep-the-old-4797537. php#/ 0.

3 Pope, Russ. Understanding Our Struggles (Kindle Locations 162-167). . Kindle Edition.

4 Jeremiah, David (2013-10-01). What Are You Afraid Of?: Facing Down Your Fears with Faith (Kindle Locations 154-157). Tyndale House Publishers, Inc.. Kindle Edition.

5 Cuyler, Theodore. God's Light on Dark Clouds (Kindle Locations 686-701). GLH Publishing. Kindle Edition

6   Jeremiah, David (2013-10-01). What Are You Afraid Of?: Facing Down Your Fears with Faith (Kindle Locations 139-141). Tyndale House Publishers, Inc.. Kindle Edition.

7   Arnold, Thomas; Maurice, F.D.; Burgon, John. Church Pulpit Commentary (12 vol. Now In One) (Kindle Locations 1951-1957). www.DelmarvaPublications.com. Kindle Edition.

8   Ibid ... (Kindle Locations 3130-3132). www.DelmarvaPublications.com. Kindle Edition.

9   Mokgoatle, Mpho; Mokgoatle, Mpho. Know yourself with the help of God (Kindle Locations 111-115). . Kindle Edition.

Chapter # 7

1   Archibald MacLeish, quoted in Sheena Iyengar, The Art of Choosing (New York: Hachette, 2010), xvii.

2   Ortberg, John. What Is God's Will for My Life? (p. 58). Tyndale House Publishers, Inc.. Kindle Edition.

3   Keyes, Dick. Beyond Identity: Finding your 'self' in the image and character of God (Kindle Locations 51-53). Destinee Media. Kindle Edition.

4   Roberson, Dave. The Walk of the Spirit - The Walk of Power: The Vital Role of Praying in Tongues (Kindle Locations 190-195). Dave Roberson Ministries. Kindle Edition.

5   Keyes, Dick. Beyond Identity: Finding your 'self' in the image and character of God (Kindle Locations 2456-2458). Destinee Media. Kindle Edition.

6   G. K. Beale. We Become What We Worship: A Biblical Theology of Idolatry (Kindle Locations 2850-2851). Kindle Edition.

7   Davis, Lynn R. How God Sees Your Struggles: Encouraging Yourself, Finding Strength And Developing A Spiritual Perspective (p. 28). Lynn R Davis. Kindle Edition.

8   Dawn, Marva J.. Being Well When We are Ill: Wholeness And Hope In Spite Of Infirmity (Living Well) (p. 131). Fortress Press. Kindle Edition.

9   Ibid ... (p. 132). Fortress Press. Kindle Edition.

10   John White, Daring to Draw Near: People in Prayer (Downers Grove: InterVarsity, 1977), 106.

11   Dawn, Marva J.. Being Well When We are Ill: Wholeness And Hope In Spite Of Infirmity (Living Well) (p. 254). Fortress Press. Kindle Edition.

Chapter # 8

1   San Pedro, Maria Ofelia Clarissa Z.; Ryan S. J. D., Baker; Ma. Mercedes T., Rodrigo (2011), "The Relationship between Carelessness and Affect in a Cognitive Tutor", Affective Computing and Intelligent Interaction, Lecture Notes in Computer Science, 6974, Berlin: Springer, pp. 306–315, ISBN 978-3-642-24599-2

2   Houge, Adam. Because He is Your Lord Worship Him (Kindle Locations 221-224). . Kindle Edition.

3   Mokgoatle, Mpho; Mokgoatle, Mpho. Know yourself with the help of God (Kindle Locations 100-104). . Kindle Edition.

4   Mokgoatle, Mpho; Mokgoatle, Mpho. Know yourself with the help of God (Kindle Locations 119-130). . Kindle Edition.

5   Ortberg, John. What Is God's Will for My Life? (p. 34). Tyndale House Publishers, Inc.. Kindle Edition.

6   Ibid … (pp. 41-42). Tyndale House Publishers, Inc.. Kindle Edition.

7   Ripken, Nik. The Insanity of Obedience: Walking with Jesus in Tough Places (p. 239). B&H Publishing Group. Kindle Edition.

8   Paul Marshall, Their Blood Cries Out (Nashville: Thomas Nelson, 1997), 4.., 249– 51.

Chapter # 9

1   Whaley, Vernon M.. Worship Through the Ages (Kindle Locations 384-388). B&H Publishing Group. Kindle Edition.

2   Ibid . . 426). .

3   Ibid . 610-644). .

4   Marti, Gerardo. Worship across the Racial Divide: Religious Music and the Multiracial Congregation (Kindle Locations 195-204). Oxford University Press. Kindle Edition.

5   Masters, Peter. Worship in the Melting Pot (Kindle Locations 280-286). . Kindle Edition.

6   Ibid 191-201

7   Ibid 211-214.

8   Ramsay, W. M.. The Letters to the Seven Churches (Kindle Locations 3100-3104). Albion Press. Kindle Edition

9   Schmidt, Ken M.. "Not Afraid To Tell the Truth" : Exposing Apostasy and the Conspiracy of Silence in the last days! (Kindle Locations 2108-2110). Xlibris. Kindle Edition.

10 Ibid 2312-2321

11 Ibid 2336-2346
12 Ibid

Chapter # 10

1   Carr, Kelly. Revelation: Book of Mystery and Majesty (p. 10). Franklin Publishing. Kindle Edition.
2   Ibid ... (p. 10). Franklin Publishing. Kindle Edition
3   Wessell, Scott. Discover Your Purpose & Calling: How To Discover What You Were Made For And Over Come The Roadblocks To Living Your Calling (Kindle Locations 99-101). IMPACT195. Kindle Edition.
4   Arnold, Thomas; Maurice, F.D.; Burgon, John. Church Pulpit Commentary (12 vol. Now In One) (Kindle Locations 68234-68236). www.DelmarvaPublications.com. Kindle Edition.
5   Ibid ... (Kindle Locations 68237-68238). www.DelmarvaPublications.com. Kindle Edition.
6   Keyes, Dick. Beyond Identity: Finding your 'self' in the image and character of God (Kindle Locations 62-67). Destinee Media. Kindle Edition.
7   Spencer, Kristin N.. You Aren't Worthless: Unlock the Truth to Godly Confidence (Kindle Locations 967-970). Sincerely Adorned Books. Kindle Edition.
8   Keyes, Dick. Beyond Identity: Finding your 'self' in the image and character of God (Kindle Locations 219-221). Destinee Media. Kindle Edition.
9   Ibid ... (Kindle Locations 1165-1172). Destinee Media. Kindle Edition.
10 Keyes, Dick. Beyond Identity: Finding your 'self' in the image and character of God (Kindle Locations 1190-1196). Destinee Media. Kindle Edition.
11 Baptist Hymnal, Edited by Walter Hines Sims; Nashville, TN: Convention Press, 1956; 238.

Chapter # 11

1   Rohrer, Susan. THE HOLY SPIRIT - Spiritual Gifts: Amazing Power for Everyday People (Illuminated Bible Study Guides Series) (p. 209). Amazon Digital Services in association with Infinite Arts Media. Kindle Edition.
2   John Calvin, Institutes of the Christian Religion, Volume 1 (Grand Rapids: Eerdmans Publishing Company, 1957), 37.
3   Saint Robert Bellarmine. A Commentary on the Book of Psalms (Illustrated) (pp. 15-16). Aeterna Press. Kindle Edition.
4   caputo, Michael. How to Prevent Your Love From becoming Cold (Kindle Locations 172-174). Ascent Educational. Kindle Edition

5   Ibid 269,274
6   Ibid 281,282
7   ibid 312,321
8   Arnold, Thomas; Maurice, F.D.; Burgon, John. Church Pulpit Commentary (12 vol. Now In One) (Kindle Locations 21282-21287). www.DelmarvaPublications.com. Kindle Edition.

Printed in the United States
By Bookmasters